THE RECKONING

How #MeToo Is Changing Australia

Jess Hill

The metallic clatter of cameras, a heavy sigh. His language emphatic: "shocked," "disgusted"; "shameful." This time he really means it. He's listening now.

By the time Prime Minister Scott Morrison fronts the press gallery in late March 2021, Australians have for more than three years been living in the era of #MeToo, and have been consuming an almost daily diet of stories about sexual harassment, assault and rape. But not stories like this. An alleged rape in a minister's office. A brutal rape alleged against the federal attorney-general. A male staffer masturbating on a female MP's desk. This is the stuff of nightmares, and it's playing out in the nation's parliament.

Morrison is hitting the bitumen to Damascus. He has been listening carefully to women about the "rubbish and crap" they have been putting up with "for their entire lives, as their mothers did, as their grandmothers did." Australian women "walk daily in fear," are "overlooked and talked over by men," are "marginalised ... belittled ... diminished ... and objectified." He bemoans the fact that women facing this behaviour in the workplace are too afraid to call it out, for fear of being intimidated or losing their job. "That's not okay," he says sincerely, "and it's not their fault. It's the environment we've allowed to be created. Whether this is unconscious deafness and blindness, or whether it is wilful malevolence that is behind all of this, it must be acknowledged, it must be called out and it must stop."

Before he's finished, Morrison asks us to grant him one indulgence. On this issue, he has the "deepest of vested interests": "Criticise me if you like for speaking about my daughters, but they are the centre of my life. My wife is the centre of my life. My mother, my widowed mother, is the centre of my life." To these four women, choking back tears, he makes his pledge: "I will not let you down." To all other women he offers encouragement and gratitude for their courage. He needs them to stand together with him.

This is the prime minister's long-awaited reset, and the mea culpa clichés are twitching in the typewriters. But then things get dark.

Andrew Clennell, political editor for Sky News Australia, asks Morrison pointedly: "Prime Minister, if you were the boss of a business and there'd been an alleged rape on your watch, and this incident we heard about last night, on your watch, your job would probably be in a bit of jeopardy, wouldn't it? Doesn't it look like you've lost control of your ministerial staff here?"

The moral and decent Dr Jekyll flips to his unrepentant double. The reporters in front of him are sitting in "glass houses," Morrison warns. Is Mr Clennell not aware of the complaint made in his own organisation, about an incident of harassment in a women's toilet? No, says Clennell, he is not.

It's a mask-off moment. Writes Luke Pearson from IndigenousX, "Just so we are all on the same page, 'Glass houses' in this context means 'We should keep each other's secrets about sexual harassment and sexual abuse in our respective workplaces' yeah? That's a very cool and normal thing for a Prime Minister to say to media live on television."

It's worse than that. The prime minister is not just making a veiled threat to the gathered reporters, and he is not just divulging a complaint made in confidence. He is sending a chilling coded message to one woman in the room: the journalist who broke the story of Brittany Higgins being

Quarterly Essay

---

1   THE RECKONING
        How #MeToo Is Changing Australia
        Jess Hill

---

132   CORRESPONDENCE
        Rachel Nolan, Bri Lee, David Hunt, Alison Pennington, Shannon Burns,
        Elizabeth Flux, Tom Lee, Vivian Gerrand, Lech Blaine

---

171   Contributors

Quarterly Essay is published four times a year by Black Inc., an imprint of Schwartz Books Pty Ltd. Publisher: Morry Schwartz.

ISBN 9781760642853 ISSN 1832-0953

All Rights Reserved.
No part of this publication may be reproduced, stored in a retrieval system, or transmitted in any form by any means electronic, mechanical, photocopying, recording or otherwise without the prior consent of the publishers.

Essay & correspondence © retained by the authors.

Subscriptions – 1 year print & digital
(4 issues): $79.95 within Australia incl. GST.
Outside Australia $119.95. 2 years print & digital
(8 issues): $149.95 within Australia incl. GST.
1 year digital only: $49.95.

Payment may be made by Mastercard or Visa, or by cheque made out to Schwartz Books. Payment includes postage and handling.

To subscribe, fill out and post the subscription card or form inside this issue, or subscribe online:

quarterlyessay.com
subscribe@blackincbooks.com
Phone: 61 3 9486 0288

Correspondence should be addressed to:

The Editor, Quarterly Essay
Level 1, 221 Drummond Street
Carlton VIC 3053 Australia
Phone: 61 3 9486 0288 / Fax: 61 3 9011 6106
Email: quarterlyessay@blackincbooks.com

Editor: Chris Feik. Management: Elisabeth Young. Publicity: Anna Lensky. Design: Guy Mirabella. Assistant Editor: Kirstie Innes-Will. Production Coordinator: Marilyn de Castro. Typesetting: Tristan Main.

Printed in Australia by McPherson's Printing Group. The paper used to produce this book comes from wood grown in sustainable forests.

allegedly raped in parliament house, News Corp's political editor, Samantha Maiden. As will emerge later, it is she against whom this "complaint" has apparently been made.

But Morrison can't even get a coded message right. There's been no complaint at News Corp, and the complaint he has invoked had nothing to do with sex or harassment; it was a disagreement about press gallery politics. The prime minister, in his passionate apology to Australian women, has just levelled a false accusation against a female journalist in the press gallery, live on national television.

Minutes earlier, he had offered this moment of communion: "Women are too afraid to call out bad behaviour for fear of losing a job or being intimidated in their workplace."

Indeed. To borrow a phrase from former prime minister Julia Gillard, what Scott Morrison needed here was not an apology, but a mirror.

Here's what men like Scott Morrison don't understand: political spin has no power against the rage unleashed by #MeToo. At its heart, this is an accountability movement, one that dares to ask men the ugly question: what will it take for your kind to stop coercing, harassing, raping, and killing women? Of power, it demands: what will it take for you to stop protecting the men who perpetrate this? To Morrison, the message is clear: passionate speeches will not appease us. *We see you.*

The cultural revolution of #MeToo is not just about sexual violence. It is taking aim at patriarchy's most sacred compact: the keeping of men's secrets. Consciousness-raising movements have for fifty years revealed the ubiquity of sexual harassment and violence. Since the rise of social media in the early 2010s, there have been viral hashtags like #YesAllWomen and #WhyIStayed. Traditionally, such movements have been focused on raising the consciousness of women, but #MeToo has taken it a step further: it has made *men* sit up and take notice. That's because, this time, women aren't just sharing what happened to them – they're pointing the finger. It's not just *I was raped*, but *he is the one who raped me* – *and they are the ones who protected him*. This approach seems to have set off an alarm bell in the amygdala of men worldwide: *holy shit, this time they're coming for us.*

For as long as we've been talking about sexual violence and domestic abuse, the men who perpetrate it have been largely invisible. Terms like "violence against women" and "women's safety" remove the perpetrator from view and foreground the victim, where she becomes the subject to interrogate: What was she wearing? Did she do something to provoke him? Why did she go back? What is she doing to keep herself safe? For decades, this polite erasure has quarantined men's violence against women in the zone of "women's issues."

In September 2021, on the first day of the National Women's Safety Summit, the almost total absence of men prompted me to pose a question on Twitter:

> I wonder how the discussions would change if instead of a #WomensSafetySummit, we had a #MensViolenceSummit? Genuine question. How would our perspectives and solutions shift if we put men's violence in the foreground?
>
> It goes like this (citing the great @jacksontkatz):
>
> John beat Mary. #MensViolenceSummit
>
> Mary was beaten by John.
>
> Mary was beaten.
>
> Mary was battered.
>
> Mary is a battered woman. #WomensSafetySummit
>
> As Katz explains, the 1st sentence is in active voice: it has a subject, a verb, & an object. A good English sentence. The 2nd is passive voice. The focus has shifted from John to Mary. The 3rd, John is invisible. By the 5th, Mary has a new identity, & "John is no longer part of the conversation."

#MeToo became a revolution, not just a movement, because it put John back at the beginning of the sentence. But keeping him there is a daily chore – and our government is doing its best to make sure we return to the passive voice.

#MeToo did not get delivered by a stork on 17 October 2017. It was born of decades of work, of bitter frustration, and a determination to prove the prevalence of sexual violence and abuse again and again and again. In this essay I track the evolution of #MeToo, how it has expressed itself in Australia and how it created the conditions for a female-led insurgency against the Morrison government in 2021.

The radical potential of #MeToo is not just in shifting norms, which can so easily regress. It's in taking this moment of normative change and making it stick: with policy, legislation, regulation and governance. It's in refusing to accept the crumbs that governments offer women. It is in the clearheadedness of journalists like 7.30's Laura Tingle, who can deny the prime minister his request for indulgence:

> Actually, Prime Minister, the women of Australia may not forgive you this indulgence. Those women may be wondering what exactly the Prime Minister has been doing for the past month and what sick culture has been allowed to develop within the Government and within Parliament House under his watch as Prime Minister since 2018.

This is the power of #MeToo. It's the power of saying No More. The power of refusing to play along. The power of putting John back at the beginning of the sentence.

#MeToo may not have taken the scalps of our most powerful, as it did in the United States. But that does not mean it has failed. In fact, as we'll see, the impact of #MeToo in Australia has been seismic.

EXPLOSION

The morning #MeToo went viral on 15 October 2017, Tarana Burke panicked. Burke, an activist and community organiser in New York, had coined the phrase twelve years earlier to connect survivors of sexual violence – mainly young black women – with each other, and build circles of safety, empathy and healing. Her work was old-school, grassroots organising. It was nothing like what was now exploding on social media. "Social media is not a safe space," she would later tell *The Guardian*. "I thought: this is going to be a fucking disaster."

The night before, on the other side of America, actress and activist Alyssa Milano had been reading about the explosive allegations of misconduct, sexual assault and rape made ten days earlier against the powerful Hollywood producer Harvey Weinstein. She was about to go to sleep when she got a text message from a friend. It contained a screenshot that read: "Suggested by a friend: if all the women who have been sexually harassed or assaulted wrote 'me too' as a status, we might give people a sense of the magnitude of the problem." Milano had never heard of Tarana Burke or her "me too" movement, but felt this act of online solidarity might reveal the shocking prevalence of sexual violence. Posting the screenshot to her millions of followers, she added: "If you've been sexually harassed or assaulted, write 'me too' as a reply to this tweet." She pressed send and went to bed. By the next morning, 55,000 people had replied. Within twenty-four hours, the hashtag would be used more than twelve million times.

Australians saw Milano's tweet go viral in real time. When it started to explode, the impact was immediate and profound. "I wrote a summary of all the 'me too' moments of my life and bawled as I wrote it," remembers author and doctor Louise Allan, "because there were so many times I'd kept my mouth shut and just put up with it. It was like opening the floodgates."

For many that afternoon, and in the days and weeks that followed, the sheer volume of disclosures from friends, family and strangers posted on their social media feeds was both exhilarating and overwhelming. "I was suddenly aware of how powerful a tool silencing has been for perpetrators of sexual assault," says Sophia Rose O'Rourke, "and [it was] like a new power had arisen. Physically I felt both constricted in my chest but desperate to speak. I just remember walking around and trying to keep up with the craziness of my day but knowing that something had changed, and I needed to stop and pay attention." Tim Baker had a kind of personal epiphany that would become a familiar one for men: "I remember it led to a conversation with my wife and discovering that she'd had all these awful experiences through her life I had no idea about and I'd been walking round oblivious to this reality half the population live with."

As Jane Campion would later describe it, #MeToo was "like the Berlin Wall coming down." Many women weren't *surprised* by the volume of disclosures, but it led many to reassess what they had lived with, been silent about, or accepted as shitty but "unavoidable." Public servant Megan O'Neill was at work that day, and she recalls the hashtag triggering a communal "purge" in her office. "Spontaneously, the women I worked with started sharing horrendous stories of sexual assaults and rape from when we were teens and through our lives. In an open-plan office. Some we hadn't thought of as sexual assault – just shit that happens to women."

For many – especially those who had for years felt alone and ashamed – the response to Milano's call-out created a feeling of instant community. "I felt like I wasn't lonely for the first time," Kayla remembers. "I thought you had to be defective for abusers to target and dehumanize you in such a way, and it was the first time I realized the problem isn't with me. I felt validated, then dreadful when I realized the problem is bigger and much more pervasive." Recalls Dr Amy Marshall, "I remember feeling validated, not just *knowing* it wasn't just me but *seeing* it wasn't just me. I tried to write all the times that I could remember, from comments to stalking to groping to rape. I lost count and cried for hours."

For some women embroiled in sexual harassment complaints, the day was a turning point. "It made my anger justifiable and righteous in a way that I had never been able to share before," recalls Ellen Stanistreet, who was enduring sexual harassment in her job from a man who had also assaulted her. "It also galvanised the people (particularly women) above me to act, when a week before they were completely unable to support me."

For others, a moment of emancipation was rear-ended by a harsh reality check. "I started thinking about the sexual assault that happened to me at fifteen and stopped blaming myself," says Spinifex Anangu and Noongar woman and doctoral researcher Aileen Marwung Walsh. "I started sharing on social media because I come from a small town. And then the women started building fences around him to protect him and other offenders."

It was also convenient cover for abusers. Ella was eighteen and in a "relationship" with the teacher who had groomed and sexually abused her in her senior year. "I didn't really understand #MeToo, mostly because I had no prior frame of reference," she says. "He read me a post he wanted to make to Facebook about the movement and his solidarity with victim-survivors; it didn't sit right with me (although I didn't know why) and I told him not to post it, and he didn't. I took it as evidence that he really loved me and wasn't abusive, but in hindsight it was all part of the abusive dynamic. Surely, better than writing a Facebook post supporting #MeToo is not perpetrating abuse? Surely."

Back in New York, as Burke scrolled anxiously, each hashtag "felt like a needle pricking my skin." Behind every single tweet – whether it was a story, an emoji or simply "#MeToo" – she could see a person in need. She was also terrified this spontaneous online movement would end up erasing hers. On the phone to friends, she cried, "This can't happen. Not like this! Y'all know if these white women start using this hashtag, and it gets popular, they will never believe that a Black woman in her forties from the Bronx has been building a movement for the *same* purposes, using these exact words, for years now. It will be over. I will have worked all these years for nothing!"

Burke was not well known, and her movement was not a hashtag. "me too." was an activist group promoting solidarity, healing, education and community; #MeToo was about solidarity too, but it was pursuing a different immediate objective: exposing powerful perpetrators. Though Burke had full respect for the women who had named Weinstein, it was never her agenda to single out individual men. She worried deeply for the wellbeing of the millions of women suddenly disclosing online. Pulling herself together, she posted a statement on Instagram:

> It has been amazing watching all of the pushback against Harvey Weinstein and in support of his accusers over the last week. In particular, today I have watched women on social media disclose their stories using the hashtag #metoo. It made my heart swell to see women using this idea – one that we call 'empowerment through empathy' – to not only show the world how widespread and pervasive sexual violence is, but also to let other survivors know they are not alone. The point of the work we've done over the last decade with the 'me too movement' is to let women, particularly young women of color, know that they are not alone – it's a movement. It's beyond a hashtag. It's the start of a larger conversation and a movement for radical community healing. Join us.

In the end, it worked. Milano gave credit to Burke, and the media – in fits and starts – eventually came to recognise Tarana Burke as the founder of the #MeToo movement. But that critical distinction between the two movements was lost – and Burke has been trying to re-establish it ever since.

Burke connected the hashtag version of #MeToo to "the work": grassroots activism, actual expertise in dealing with sexual violence, and the mission of structural change. Her collectivist approach – and her centring of marginalised survivors – gave the hashtag its soul and, I'd argue, has guaranteed its longevity.

But for better or worse, the hashtag version of #MeToo that was now ascendant was inextricably linked to the extraordinary demise of Harvey Weinstein and the mostly white celebrities who accused him. For many, that was its genesis story – and in the public mind, that shaped both its meaning and its measure of success. The Weinstein exposé created a template for taking down powerful men – and big scalps would become the criterion by which the movement's success was judged. The cultural revolution triggered by #MeToo was, at least in its initial phase, not in line with Burke's vision of healing and structural change: it was about rage and retribution.

*

When the stories about Harvey Weinstein broke in October 2017, first in *The New York Times* and then in *The New Yorker*, the impact was seismic. This was one of Hollywood's most powerful producers, and a major donor to women's rights organisations, progressive causes and the Democratic Party. It was not just his serial sexual predation that shocked the public (in time, more than eighty women would come forward with allegations of harassment, assault and rape), but the supporting cast of individuals, systems and institutions that had enabled and protected him for decades. Weinstein's sexual predation had been an open secret for years, and journalists had attempted to report on it several times. Such was the ring of steel around Weinstein that Ronan Farrow had to resign from NBC just so he could get his story published (in *The New Yorker*).

When Weinstein's protection was ripped away, it was as if someone had disabled a forcefield. "The protective cladding of power and privilege that had long silenced victims and shielded powerful perpetrators had been pierced," wrote journalist Kristine Ziwica. "You could hear the alarm bells in Hollywood and around the world: *beep, beep – rape-culture systems are down.*"

This was a rare moment of structural weakness in patriarchy: a vulnerable piece of flesh had been exposed, and it was as though women all over the world received a subliminal message that now was the time to draw back their arrows and shoot. The army they were joining wasn't just one of ordinary women, but *famous* women with "perfect" lives. These women were disavowing the shame of being preyed on and putting it back where it belonged: with the men who harmed them. The disclosures and solidarity expressed by celebrities such as Salma Hayek, Gwyneth Paltrow,

Lady Gaga, Uma Thurman and Ashley Judd offered cultural protection to other victim-survivors – yes, like them, I also: #MeToo.

Yet #MeToo did not just appear out of thin air, and though boosted by Hollywood, it did not originate there. Instead, it was a firestorm produced by a slow-building weather system; a gradual increase in heat, frequency and severity that accumulated over years. At its centre was the raging sense of injustice felt by victims who had been abused by powerful and untouchable men; victims who had been reflexively disbelieved, or – worse still – treated like fantasists, especially if they tried to reveal systematic cover-ups. It seems hard to believe now, but most people could not or *would not* believe that well-regarded men in powerful positions would commit sexual violence, and it was unimaginable that trusted institutions would protect and enable them.

The gradual build-up to #MeToo was marked by particular factors: from an acceleration in the exposure of powerful predators (and the systems that protected them) to a fundamental shift in how we perceived victims, and a growing awareness of the injustice at the core of our justice systems. In other words, just as climate change does not *cause* heatwaves or fires but creates the conditions for heatwaves to become more intense and fires to burn more fiercely, the Weinstein exposé did not *cause* a revolution against men's sexual violence. Rather, a confluence of accelerating events set the stage for it.

It's important, before we get to Australia, to understand how this weather system was formed. That means looking, firstly, to the United States, where – a decade after Anita Hill accused Supreme Court nominee Clarence Thomas of sexual harassment – it really started to build in the early 2000s, with *The Boston Globe*'s "Spotlight" investigation into child sex abuse within the Catholic Church. Since the 1980s, the media had reported on paedophile priests internationally, but this ground-breaking investigation provided incontrovertible evidence that these men were not acting alone; they were protected and enabled by senior church leadership, who conspired with police to silence victims, settled claims privately, and quietly moved offending priests from parish to parish. The *Globe*'s reporting "put a match to some very, very dry tinder," and triggered an avalanche of reporting around the world, exposing endemic paedophilia, sadistic child abuse and systematic concealment of child sex crimes within the Catholic Church.

This revelation didn't just violate the trust of believers; it landed the unbearable idea that these "good men" in authority – God's own emissaries on earth – were not just capable of sadistic sexual violence, they were *prone* to it. But for the time being, this horrible realisation was confined to the realms of churches and children. As a society, we were yet to grapple with the ubiquity of sexual violence and its intimate relationship with power more broadly. But that was coming.

In 2011, Nafissatou Diallo, a single parent living in the Bronx, reported the head of the International Monetary Fund to the police for violently raping her. Her case was, in the eyes of author and feminist Rebecca Solnit, "a shaking of the foundations." "In an earlier era, her word would have been worthless against his and she might not have filed charges, or the police might not have followed through and yanked Dominique Strauss-Kahn off a plane to Paris at the last moment." Kahn was not convicted, but he settled with Diallo in the civil courts for an undisclosed sum. That wasn't the end of it: Diallo's courage emboldened other women to come forward and it emerged that Kahn was notorious for his "predatory behaviour towards women and his sexual pursuit of them, from students and journalists to subordinates." The scandal ended Kahn's political career: he quit the IMF, gave up on a run for the French presidency and withdrew from public life.

Still, Kahn was believed to be a one-off weather event, a freak occurrence. In the public mind, he was packed away into the carton of "bad eggs."

The next weather event was more cataclysmic, and lit up not just a single predator, but a network of institutions. In October 2012, posthumous revelations about one of Britain's most iconic celebrities, Jimmy Savile (a prolific fundraiser, like Weinstein), revealed the former children's television host had sexually abused an estimated 450 people over six decades. Using his fame and charitable work for hospitals to gain unsupervised access to patients, the diabolical Savile raped and sexually abused "boys, girls, men and women aged between five and seventy-five in wards, corridors and offices. Some of the victims were attacked as they lay on hospital trolleys after operations." Rumours about Savile had been circulating for decades, but, in a story familiar to Australians, allegations had been silenced by the UK's strict defamation laws. When the story finally broke, it "transformed how we deal with allegations of sexual assault," wrote Jonathan Maitland. "We reassessed our attitude to celebrity. We saw more clearly than ever how morally corrupt institutions could be." On display was not just the depravity of Savile, but the complicity of the institutions he groomed: "the BBC, the NHS, the Catholic church, the police, the government – in the shape of Mrs Thatcher – and the monarchy. (The Prince of Wales called Savile his 'health adviser')." It also gave other victim-survivors a template to follow, and gradually they too began to tell secrets they'd been keeping for decades, including stories of sexual violence perpetrated by other high-profile figures.

In 2013, Operation Yewtree – established in the wake of Savile to unearth serial predators – trained its eyes on Australia's own Rolf Harris (musician, artist and – again – children's television host). In 2014, Harris was found guilty of assaulting four girls, aged nine to nineteen, and sentenced to jail for five years and nine months. The then prime minister, Tony Abbott, felt "gutted and dismayed," and said, "it's important that we do everything we can to protect vulnerable young people. Sexual abuse is an abhorrent crime." But don't worry, everybody, Rolf was just another bad egg. Said Abbott: "It's just sad and tragic that this person who was admired seems to have been a perpetrator." As Abbott made those remarks, his own spiritual mentor, George Pell, was being questioned by the Royal Commission about what he had known about abuse by clergy.

As these weather events joined up, they also became more frequent – and started to reveal a pattern. 2014 marked a tipping point. When a White

House task force found that one in five women had been sexually assaulted in college, Vice President Joe Biden didn't mince words: "You don't want to be a school that mishandles rape. Guess what? Step up. It's time." A month later, Elliot Rodger – a self-proclaimed "incel" – went on a murderous rampage near the University of California. He left behind a chilling manifesto, in which he railed against the "sluts" who refused to have sex with him, and the men who were taking what he deserved. "The girls don't flock to the gentlemen. They flock to the alpha male," Rodger wrote. "Who's the alpha male now, bitches?"

For women worldwide, Rodger's misogynistic screed was all too familiar: it echoed the threats of rape and violence many received on social media from trolls who wanted to terrify them into silence. Predictably, one of these men had picked up a gun and followed through. The hashtag #YesAllWomen became a rallying point: used more than a million times to deluge the #NotAllMen crowd in a torrent of posts about the everyday fear, harassment, threats and violence experienced by women. Later that year, another hashtag – #WhyIStayed – drew survivors of domestic abuse into a wave of online truth-telling.

In 2015, another iconic performer, comedian and sitcom star Bill Cosby, was accused of rape by forty-six women. Sexual assault allegations had already been made by fourteen women in 2005, but "no one wanted to believe the TV dad in a cardigan was capable of such things, and so they didn't." They didn't have to. As one accuser, Tamara Green, said, "In 2005, Bill Cosby still had control of the media." A decade later, social media had changed everything: "We can't be disappeared. It's online and can never go away." Forty-six women from ten states: supermodels, waitresses, journalists, Playboy bunnies and staffers in the entertainment industry. Critically, they did not remain anonymous: thirty-five agreed to be photographed for the cover of *New York Magazine*. Their testimonies revealed Cosby's modus operandi: in almost every assault, he drugged a woman with Quaaludes and, once she was physically immobilised, raped her. The last thing many of these women remembered was being handed a drink, blacking out and waking up with him "forcing himself into my mouth," "seeing semen on the floor," climbing on top of them, digitally penetrating them. Chelan Lasha, who was seventeen when Cosby assaulted her, blacked out with him humping her leg; when she woke up thirteen hours later, he was standing above her, clapping his hands and shouting, "Daddy says, wake up!" For a time, she feared for her life, due to Cosby's influence. It was thirty years before she came forward.

This intense reckoning with men's sexual violence was paving the way for another precondition for #MeToo: the humanisation of female victims and, perhaps for the first time, an interest in hearing from them directly. Two women shaped the Australian build-up to #MeToo: domestic abuse survivor Rosie Batty, who was named Australian of the Year in 2015; and American rape survivor Chanel Miller, known originally as "Emily Doe," whose victim impact statement went viral around the world. Both used the platform they had – Batty on the national stage, Miller in the courtroom – to demolish myths about domestic abuse and rape, and to transmit the visceral lived experience of men's violence, and what happens when that is ignored or colluded with by the state.

In Australia, Batty assumed the role of a modern-day Cassandra. Like countless victims before her, her warnings about a violent man had been "minimised, dismissed, believed, acted on and then lost in the system." Unlike most victims, though, the horrifying consequence of this was realised "not behind closed doors ... but in front of children and parents on a public cricket ground." Her colossal grief was channelled into a nation-stopping moment on an ordinary Australian street – and it finally gave a familiar refrain the power to breach our collective denial. "Family violence happens to everybody, no matter how nice your house is, how intelligent you are. It happens to everyone and anyone." Suddenly, the tables were turned: we wanted to hear from victims of domestic abuse. We were interested in their stories. We needed to understand.

If Batty created a platform for survivors of men's violence, Chanel Miller provided a manifesto. The week before Batty was named Australian of the

Year, Miller was raped on campus at Stanford University in California. Two male grad students saw Brock Turner raping Miller near a dumpster; when they saw that she seemed to be unconscious, they chased a fleeing Turner, tackled him to the ground and held him until police could arrive. This was a rare circumstance: a witnessed rape. Even rarer, Turner was convicted. And yet, the headlines that followed the case described him as an "All-American swimmer," and Miller, as she later recalled, "as an unconscious intoxicated woman – ten syllables, and nothing more than that." In June 2016, at Turner's sentencing hearing, "Emily Doe" looked directly at the man who raped her and read out her victim impact statement: "You don't know me, but you've been inside me, and that's why we're here today," she began. Her statement – all 7244 words – was published online by *Buzzfeed*. In four days, the article had four million hits. Not only did Miller articulate the horror of the rape and its aftermath, but she clinically debunked the legal strategies used against her and practically every rape survivor. Journalist and survivor advocate Nina Funnell, who would later create the #LetHerSpeak campaign, wrote:

> she is radically rewriting ideas about victimhood. In the cultural conscience, victims are often presented as broken, voiceless and downtrodden. At best, we are pitied. At worst, we are despised and devalued as "damaged goods." Yet through her victim impact statement she has ... advanced a new image of a survivor who is intelligent, articulate, analytical, insightful, bold, brave, reflective and persuasive.

Miller's statement was read in its entirety on the floor of the US Congress and on CNN. Her voice was centred in this story, and a very different kind of attention was paid to the man who raped her. In a letter that also went viral, Turner's father lamented the price his son had to pay for "20 minutes of action." But when Brock Turner received a two-month sentence from a judge concerned for his future career prospects, he was struck by a tidal wave of global fury. As Kasey Edwards wrote for *The Sydney Morning Herald*, this rape had not been caused by alcohol, but by "Turner's sense of entitlement; the belief that women are toys – or even prey – rather than people, and that he should be able to play with or hunt them without consequence."

The ferocity and frequency of extreme rape culture events was accelerating. Within five months of Miller's statement, the world had a new predator-in-chief – an archetypal patriarch whose ascension to the White House was not impeded by his admission on tape that he grabbed women "by the pussy" because "when you're a star, they let you do it." When he saw a beautiful woman, Donald Trump told a sniggering Billy Bush, "I just start kissing them. It's like a magnet. Just kiss – I don't even wait." Caught on a hot mic, here was one of the world's most powerful men, whose wife was pregnant, clearly stating that he consciously and strategically sexually assaulted women – and other men were laughing along with him. It was a mask-off moment, and, as Maureen Ryan wrote for *Vanity Fair*, "when the *Access Hollywood* tape dropped, women in all industries and workplaces could point to it as proof of the misogyny and (white) boys-club atmosphere that they so often faced."

Many were convinced that the pussy-grabbing tape had ended Trump's presidential run. But on 4 November 2016, not only was Trump elected, but CNN exit polls revealed that 53 per cent of white women had voted for him. (By contrast, 94 per cent of black women and 68 per cent of Latino women voted for Hillary Clinton.) The awful truth was that Trump was elected not just despite this tape, but "quite possibly *because of it*: because of his bellicose racism, sexism, and xenophobia," wrote Ryan.

On election day, I went to a US Studies Centre party at Manning Bar in Sydney University. My brother was with me and, convinced Clinton was about to win, he thought it might be funny to stand with the bellicose male students in the Trump corner. As states fell to Trump one by one, the MAGA hat–wearing young men grew increasingly raucous, chanting "drain the swamp," "lock her up" and "build that wall." As it became clear that Trump was about to clinch the crucial state of Ohio, one of them shouted: "Grab 'em by the pussy! That's how we do it!"

This was the masculinity now in ascendancy. I walked off campus sobbing with rage. A narcissistic, racist misogynist now led the "free world," and I despaired for the little life that had just begun to grow inside me.

What was not obvious that afternoon was that the election of Donald Trump was the next big tipping point. The day after Trump's inauguration in January 2017, more than 470,000 people descended on Washington DC for the Women's March, said to be the biggest single-day protest in American history. Nationwide, protests drew as many as five million people to more than 400 demonstrations; and there were hundreds of women's marches on every continent, including Australia.

The rage over Trump gave a shot of electricity to a number of dormant movements, including Black Lives Matter. For feminism – which had just start to crest into a third wave – Trump's election showed that not only was the work far from done, the "ugly underbelly of persistent sexism" and racism had never gone away. "Trump has reinvigorated feminism and the women's movement," wrote American journalist Jodi Enda, "in a way that nothing has done for decades."

When the Weinstein stories dropped in October 2017 – almost a year to the day after the pussy-grabbing tape – all the necessary conditions for a firestorm were in place. The Weinstein story began a process that would bust through our doublethink on sexual violence – that we could both know the statistics *and* operate on the basis that they may not be true. We were about to reckon with the fact that sexual violence is not just prevalent, but endemic.

Once #MeToo went viral, powerful men across the United States started dropping like flies. It's easy to forget what this period was like; we've been living in the #MeToo era for more than four years and we're not as shocked now when a famous man – even one we "like" or admire – is accused of sexual misconduct. But after the Weinstein story broke, the sheer volume of accusations levelled against famous (and often revered) men was breathtaking. In the first six months of #MeToo, credible and often career-ending claims of sexual harassment, abuse or rape were made against: the *Today*

Show's Matt Lauer (sexual harassment/assault); CBS stalwart Charlie Rose (sexual harassment and bullying); senior vice president at NPR Michael Oreskes (sexual harassment); former president George H.W. Bush (groping); *Rolling Stone* publisher Jann Wenner (sexual harassment/assault and unwanted touching); prominent physics professor (and regular ABC guest) Lawrence Krauss (groping and inappropriate behaviour); *National Enquirer* editor Dylan Howard (sexual harassment); rapper Nelly (sexual assault); R&B singer R. Kelly (convicted this year on charges of racketeering and sex trafficking); powerful literary editor Leon Wieseltier (sexual harassment); directors Oliver Stone (groping), Lars von Trier (sexual harassment), Morgan Spurlock (rape and sexual harassment), Bryan Singer (rape) and Brett Ratner (sexual harassment/assault); actors Kevin Spacey (sexual harassment/assault and sexual advances towards underage boys), Sylvester Stallone (sexual assault), Richard Dreyfuss (sexual harassment), Jeffrey Tambor (sexual harassment, forced kissing), Michael Douglas (sexual harassment and masturbation), Casey Affleck (sexual harassment), Dustin Hoffman (sexual harassment/assault) and James Franco (sexually exploitative behaviour); porn star Ron Jeremy (rape, sexual assault, unwanted touching); photographers Mario Testino (groping, masturbation, unwanted advances), Bruce Weber (unwanted touching) and Patrick Demarchelier (unwanted advances); magician David Copperfield (sexual assault); music executive Russell Simmons (rape/sexual and physical assault); Republican Senate candidate Roy Moore (preying on underage girls); and comedian Louis CK (sexual harassment and public masturbation).

For several months, one's morning routine consisted of waking up, grabbing a coffee and catching up on which of your artistic heroes had been exposed as a sexual deviant overnight. In the corporate world too, serial predators were finally being fired: within eighteen months, 414 high-profile corporate executives and business leaders were outed, all but seven of them men. Even the official pursuing Harvey Weinstein in the courts, New York State attorney-general Eric Schneiderman – an outspoken advocate for survivors – was forced to resign after four women reported he had violently abused them during his tenure. "I *am* the law," he reportedly told one, threatening her to stay quiet.

There was no getting around it: #MeToo was now an accountability movement, and its success was being measured by how many powerful men it was able to expose. It was not looking to expose sexual harassment by bartenders and factory workers – it was, as British sociologist Jeff Hearn writes, a distinct form of activism seeking to root out powerful offenders – "omnipotent male perpetrators" – who had exploited their position. Media companies, which had ignored and blocked such stories for years, were now falling over themselves to land the next big fish.

In Australia, the extraordinary energy and heat generated in the first twenty-four hours of #MeToo was almost immediately channelled into that same narrow project: unmasking famous and powerful predators. On 18 October 2017, the former newsreader Tracey Spicer tweeted: "Currently, I am investigating two long-term offenders in our media industry. Please, contact me privately to tell your stories." Spicer wasn't just hungry for a scoop. With her memoir *The Good Girl Stripped Bare*, she had reinvented herself as a high-profile feminist, crusading against sexism and discrimination in the media. The idea for her tweet had come to her at Manly Police Station, where she'd gone to report the latest batch of misogynistic abuse posted on her Facebook page. Many were threats of sexual violence from "Australian men whose Facebook accounts showed them relaxing in pleasant suburban homes, playing with grandchildren and hugging their wives." The female detective to whom she was reporting made an offhand remark about the Weinstein story, "and how rare it was for Australian women to approach police about abuse and harassment." That got Spicer thinking: who were Australia's notorious media men?

Top of her list was Don Burke. By November, out of around 870 responses, fifty concerned Burke. The sheer volume of allegations, combined with his profile, made him the ideal subject for the first Australian exposé. The resulting stories – a co-production between the ABC and *The Age/Sydney Morning Herald* – delivered a hammer blow to Burke's reputation. Not only did more than fifty former colleagues label him "a 'psychotic bully,' a 'misogynist' and a 'sexual predator' who indecently assaulted, sexually harassed and bullied a string of female employees," senior male executives at Nine went on the record confirming his reputation as a "grub." Said David Leckie, the former chief executive of the Nine Network: "I've been trying to think of Harvey Weinstein-type people [in Australia] and the only one I can ever come up with is Burke. He was a horrible, horrible man." It was simple now for Burke's former bosses to disown him; his show had been axed in 2004. As one former staffer told *The Sydney Morning Herald*, "Every single person in management ... has known about Don Burke. Every male manager. There is not one that does not know." In fact, management had apparently told staff to "suck it up, because [*Burke's Backyard*] was the No.1 rating show, the cash cow for Channel Nine."

The exhaustive work carried out by esteemed investigative journalists Kate McClymont and Lorna Knowles, as well as Tracey Spicer and Alison Branley, left no room for Burke to sue. They had a watertight truth defence, and he knew it. There was a televised interview, a tawdry attempt to pin his bad behaviour on being autistic, and that was it.

The potential to keep rolling out #MeToo exposés seemed, at this stage, limitless. But by late November, the Murdoch papers hadn't managed to land one #MeToo story. Desperate for a scoop, but with little more to go on than a second-hand report of an internal complaint, they went large on the front page of *The Daily Telegraph*. There, looking forlorn and haggard in white face paint as King Lear, was the beloved actor Geoffrey Rush and the headline "King Leer." The story offered vague details about Rush being accused of inappropriate behaviour by an unnamed complainant (later revealed to be the actor Eryn Jean Norvill, who never consented to her complaint being published). Unsurprisingly, Rush announced the following week that he was suing for defamation. Norvill was left in an invidious position: remain quiet and allow Rush to clear his "good name," or go public and be subjected to an arduous court process. To her credit, Norvill agreed to be a witness, at enormous risk to her career and reputation, to prevent Rush from repeating the behaviour she alleged had occurred.

The *Telegraph* played fast and loose with Norvill's private complaint against Rush. It was a story they put together based on rumours and hearsay. The *Telegraph* knew that even with Norvill agreeing to be a witness, it did not have a strong enough case. It had to find more complainants, and fast. One person it went to was employment lawyer Josh Bornstein from Maurice Blackburn, who had acted in some of the country's highest-profile sexual harassment cases. "They rang me when they were in the middle of the defamation trial with Geoffrey Rush, desperate to see whether I had any cases against him so that they could introduce them to the defence," says Bornstein. "Bit late, fuckwits."

Principal at Marque Lawyers Michael Bradley says that suing for defamation is actually a "high-risk" strategy for a man publicly accused of sexual harassment or assault. "But the *Telegraph* just put it in his lap and gave him an unlosable case."

Bradley knows what it takes to defamation-proof a #MeToo story. He worked closely with journalist and survivor advocate Nina Funnell (as well as Chris Graham) to prepare the *New Matilda* exposé of one of Australia's highest-profile barristers, Charles Waterstreet, in October 2017. "The only way to get these stories up is to prepare them for trial. You have to prepare the story as if you're preparing your defence. Those complainants in the Waterstreet case; we prepared them like we prepare witnesses. We took detailed statements, sworn evidence from them, we did all the investigating to get whatever evidence was available to back up their stories. We literally prepared it like a brief for going to war." The result? Waterstreet wrote a spirited defence denying the allegations in *The Sydney Morning Herald*, but did not sue.

There's no doubt that Australian defamation laws are strict – and far stricter than those in the United States. For public figures, US libel cases place the burden most heavily on the claimant, who must prove that the publisher was motivated by "actual malice." Australian defamation laws, described in *The New York Times* as "oppressive and notoriously complex," place the burden on the publisher, requiring them not only to prove the material is true, but also that the "defamatory stings" – the conclusions likely to be drawn by the reader about that person – can be substantiated. In sexual harassment cases, which are commonly based on the accuser's testimony, this can be a very challenging bar to jump.

Bradley explains: "The textbook example of how to do it was the Don Burke one, which was really a replication of the Weinstein approach: bury him in volume, so he knows that there's no point – he's done. There's a tipping point, and it's a game of bluff, right? [By contrast, actor] Craig McLachlan took the other course: call the bluff. He went after them *and* sued one of the victims."

It was the Rush case specifically that "scared the shit out of everyone. It was just such a game-changer," Bradley says. "If that hadn't happened, if they'd done their homework properly ... I know that Fairfax and ABC had a queue of stories lining up they were going to run. Everyone just ran for the exit. It stopped the whole thing dead in its tracks."

In the wake of Justice Wigney's decision to award Rush $850,000 in damages, News Corp positioned itself as a crusader for press freedom. At a breakfast hosted by Twitter, and sitting alongside former Al Jazeera reporter Peter Greste and investigative journalist Kate McClymont, News Corp's in-house counsel Michael Cameron decried Australia's defamation laws. "If it wasn't for journalists, Harvey Weinstein would still be producing films. If the Weinstein story had come out in Australia, he would be suing you and probably would have a good chance of winning."

Let me put a finer point on Cameron's statement. If the Weinstein story had been revealed by *The Daily Telegraph* – and if they didn't bother to get any of his actual victims speaking on *or* off the record – Weinstein would still be producing films. Let's be clear: the *Telegraph*'s story on Rush was an epic failure of journalistic ethics – by far the most egregious example of "trial by media" in Australia's #MeToo era. What Cameron should have done on that panel was apologise – to Eryn Jean Norvill, and to hardworking journalists who would now, thanks to News Corp's sloppy "gotcha" journalism, struggle mightily to publish the #MeToo exposés sitting in their notepads.

Nina Funnell not only reported the Waterstreet exposé but executed the #LetHerSpeak campaign, which required years of reporting, advocacy and legal challenges to overturn several laws gagging sexual assault victims. She's clear on this point: defamation laws are "bad, and they need to change, but they didn't derail the movement."

Bradley believes that, had the media continued to roll out high-profile stories in a careful, methodical way, the momentum may have overwhelmed the *Defamation Act*. But thanks to the Rush case, that will always be a hypothetical.

*

In any case, blaming defamation laws for derailing the movement is missing the point. Was #MeToo really only about outing famous predators? If we were acknowledging Tarana Burke as the founder of the movement, why were we not measuring its success against her criteria? There was a tension developing here – two movements had been conjoined as one, and the important distinctions between them lost. The same people who would rush to acknowledge Burke's founding of #MeToo would, in the next breath, emphasise the need to expose high-profile predators – which Burke saw as being almost contrary to her mission.

Speaking in Australia in 2018, Burke tried to counter the building narrative. While local defamation laws were "monstrous," she said, "We can't get caught up in that being the thing that is holding the movement back here. There are lots of ways to talk about the work that don't defame anyone ... that talk about the systems."

Appearing at various events alongside Tracey Spicer, who was by then presenting herself as having "spearheaded" Australia's #MeToo movement, Burke seemed weary of the focus on individual perpetrators. She made the same point again and again: "This is not a movement about simply calling out individual bad actors, but the global health crisis of sexual violence ...

But still the focus for a lot of media outlets is on: who will be next, instead of who is coming forward … and who isn't."

Speaking in November 2018, a year after #MeToo went viral, Burke told a conference in Florida that the movement was at times "unrecognisable" to her.

> My vision for the Me Too movement is part of a collective vision to see a world free of sexual violence. I believe we can build that world. Full stop. We start by dismantling the building blocks of sexual violence: power and privilege. This starts by shifting our culture away from a focus on individual bad actors or depraved, isolated behaviour.
>
> Instead, we must recognize that any person sitting in a position of power comes with privilege, rendering those without power vulnerable – whether it's a boss and employee, coach and athlete, landlord and tenant or another similar dynamic.

There's no doubt that the outing of high-profile men gave – and continues to give – #MeToo much of its cultural power. These are watershed events that change cultural norms, and indicate that the age of impunity for men is – if not quite over – in its twilight. But there's a fine line between holding men publicly accountable and getting bogged down in a game of Whac-A-Mole, in which individual women are required time and again to step into the media glare and name their perpetrator. It trains our attention on scandal, but not necessarily on reforms required to stop them from happening. For #MeToo to endure as a cultural force, it would need to take what it had achieved in the theatre of accountability, and go backstage where the real work is done: to change policy, legislation and governance.

So when we talk about #MeToo, it's vital to understand that we're describing two distinct movements. The Tarana Burke movement "me too.," which is focused on solidarity and healing for survivors as well as structural change; and the Milano hashtag #MeToo, which is characterised by the drive to expose powerful predators and the systems that protect them. But the two movements, though operating in tension with each other, have also been symbiotic: Burke's movement may never have come to the world's attention without the Milano hashtag, and Milano's hashtag would likely never have found its longevity and sense of mission without Burke. Without their fusion, we may have seen a few powerful men forced to resign, but the structures that underpin their behaviours may not have felt the merest tremor. The individual perpetrators would likely have gone to ground, run to their lawyers, intimidated their victims and weathered the storm. Burke gave the movement its backbone and connected it back to the grassroots. From the beginning, she has kept the bigger project firmly in #MeToo's sights.

"People ask, 'In four years, what has Me Too done?' What people mean by that is they're taking score," Tarana Burke told *The New York Times* in 2021. "'Oh, well, you had [New York Governor Andrew] Cuomo. That's, you know, one for you. Oh, Cosby got let out ... That's one you lost.' And I'm like, 'The question is: What has MeToo made possible?'"

AWAKENING

> What would happen if one woman told the truth about her life?
> The world would split open.
>
> —Muriel Rukeyser

As #MeToo crashed into 2018, it became clear that unlike other viral hashtags, this one was not about to flame out. In almost every corner of the world, it was injecting momentum into existing movements against men's violence and adapting to local conditions.

In Japan – a deeply sexist country with a strong aversion to public shaming, where there are no laws against sexual harassment and only 4 per cent of rape victims go to police – the culture wasn't ready for the West's version of #MeToo. Instead, it started softly as #WeToo, in which company representatives declared their workplaces harassment-free, and #KuToo (a pun on *kutsu*, meaning shoes, and *kutsuu*, "pain" or "suffering"), which sought to ban companies from forcing women to wear high heels to work. By April 2018, this tentative movement had taken root firmly enough to force the resignation of one of Japan's most senior bureaucrats over sexual misconduct.

The Muslim world saw another adaptation: #MosqueMeToo, coined by the Egyptian-American feminist Mona Eltahawy. Women from Pakistan to Indonesia shared stories of sexual assault inside mosques. In Iran, where protests were taking off against compulsory hijab laws, the flood of #MosqueMeToo disclosures gave the movement the evidence it needed to persist: "Men and women wanted to use the hashtag to say 'See, when they say cover yourself, sister, to be safe, it doesn't work,'" explained BBC journalist Faranak Amidi. "If you are saying, I was in the holiest place on earth [the Hajj] and I got groped, then that's not holy, is it?" #MosqueMeToo was not just exposing sexual violence – it was questioning the very foundations of the Islamic state. "It is very, very radical," she told the BBC. "There is no way you can go back to the world before #MeToo."

In Australia, the #MeToo movement was umbilically connected to the one unfolding in the United States. Intent on replicating its high-octane accountability movement, we waited with bated breath for the whisper network to shed its secrets. Unlike other countries, we didn't realise we would need to adapt #MeToo to our own cultural conditions: our unreconstructed sexism, our national obsession with secrecy, and the tightness of our elite power networks. Instead, anointed as leader of Australia's #MeToo was the woman promising a redux of America's Weinstein moment: Tracey Spicer.

When Spicer's quest to spike Australia's "shitty media men" fell over in the wake of the *Telegraph*'s Geoffrey Rush debacle, her attention turned to establishing an organisation in the mould of America's #TimesUp. NOW Australia, launched in March 2018, promised a "triage service" of free legal support and counselling to victims of workplace sexual harassment and abuse. Spicer felt she'd diagnosed the root problem for female sexual assault victims in Australia: they didn't know where to go. This wasn't based on consultations with the sector but on her own anecdotal experience – she had received thousands of disclosures from women who didn't seem to know where else to turn.

Spicer quickly became the #MeToo talking head of choice. As a result, #MeToo from the outset became less about a collective movement and more about one individual – who would then be regarded as a gatekeeper.

The wheels started to come off almost as soon as they were bolted on. A now infamous cover of the corporate women's magazine *Latte* featured Spicer, strong and defiant, at the centre of a circle of mostly white women in power suits, above the headline, "This Ends Now: Tracey Spicer and the women dismantling discrimination." The problem was not just, as Darug woman and writer Laura La Rosa would tell *Buzzfeed*, that NOW was presented as "glaringly white and middle-class," but that Spicer was wedging a collectivist movement into the prism of corporate feminism. A nationwide tour touted by the magazine, at $139 a head, promised to transform attendees into "outspoken women" with Spicer's advice on body language and social media, as well as tips for those who'd been silenced or sacked due to harassment and discrimination. NOW Board director Nareen Young — a leading expert on workplace governance and diversity, with decades of experience in collective organising — was "beyond furious," tweeting that she had not known about the cover story, and that what was offered up was "shameful and embarrassing." Overall, says Young, the problem was that Spicer didn't give "an ounce of consideration to the mainstream notion of diversity in this country. I think that's who's missed out, and that the #MeToo movement, as it's developed, is about corporate feminism, and what happens in corporates. I think there's a lot of room for there to be other discussions."

Young was the canary in the coalmine. Over the following months, NOW would slowly disintegrate and Spicer soon became the subject of rolling controversy. Investigations by *Buzzfeed* and News.com.au would reveal that she had resisted urgings to consult with the sexual violence sector and had promised a service that would be impossible to provide. The resources required to provide free counselling and legal advice to the limitless pool of sexual violence victims in Australia were way out of NOW's reach. Spicer would eventually go to ground, saying she'd been diagnosed with a major depressive disorder as a result of vicarious trauma. Later, in an ironic twist, this same critic of Australia's harsh defamation laws — which "protect the rich and powerful" — threatened to sue former colleagues and even a survivor for criticising her publicly.

Worse still, the impossible promises Spicer made — that she would reply to every survivor who contacted her with allegations — ended up causing great harm to women whose emails she ignored. Dhanya Mani was a NSW Liberal Party political staffer who had an allegation to disclose: that she'd been sexually assaulted by a fellow staffer. She emailed Spicer in May 2018, having gleaned from the extensive media coverage that anyone seeking to engage with the #MeToo movement in Australia would have to go through its leader. Seeing that Spicer was working alongside academics and other advocates for people of colour, Mani was reassured — "perhaps," she thought, "this is something I can trust." Months went by without a reply;

Spicer would later say that her Fairfax email had been "shut down." Eventually, "through therapy and sheer force of will," Mani was able to convince herself that her story *was* important, and told it to *The Sydney Morning Herald*. Mani went to Spicer for an apology. "I had to drag the words, 'I'm sorry' out of her," she tells me, "and they came packaged in coercive language around her mental health, making me feel responsible for her potential suicidal thoughts." Spicer asked Mani to promise, in writing, that she would stop critiquing her publicly.

The Spicer era of #MeToo in Australia consumed much of its first year. Many advocates are still angry that this generative time – full of unprecedented heat and momentum and promise – was wasted. "It felt a bit like that moment got taken," says Sharna Bremner, founder of End Rape on Campus Australia. "It was a one-off moment that we would never really get again." Nina Funnell, who described NOW as "the great feminist Fyre Festival" – big on fancy Instagram influencers, media tiles and branded merchandise, but lacking in grassroots consultation – is more direct. "From my perspective, the #MeToo movement in Australia has been absolutely vacuous," she says. "I really have nothing positive to say about it."

The failing was not Spicer's alone. In every country it touched, #MeToo gave momentum to the dominant form of feminism: in Australia, that was corporate feminism. There *was* no substantial collectivist movement ready to lead #MeToo when it happened – and Spicer filled the vacuum.

"If something happens in the arena of environment or climate, the movement is ready to go," says Abbey Kendall, director of the South Australian Working Women's Centre. "They are well-organised and can respond quickly to political decisions and or big events. We don't have an equivalent advocacy movement of that scale around women and sexual violence." Instead, the enormous movement dedicated to fighting sexual violence is consumed almost entirely with crisis response; for many, advocacy is something that gets added on to an already crushing caseload. Unions work on these issues every day and continue to improve conditions for women in the workplace. But as a movement, feminism has strayed a long way from the organised collectives of the 1970s. Mani says that if feminists want to achieve structural change, this kind of old-fashioned political organising is essential. "Many feminists take pride in disavowing activism that engages with politics. I find that absurd – how the fuck are you meant to get change and legislative reform for women if you aren't engaging with politics? We need to accept that feminism is a political movement, and one that needs structure and representation."

In many ways, the real work started once Spicer's personality-led movement had been dispatched with. Thankfully, beneath the scandals, the politics and the false starts, the reckoning of #MeToo was too powerful to be squandered. Instead, it signalled a cultural awakening that would, over the following years, spark up intermittently, before leading eventually to another moment of conflagration.

*

The awakening #MeToo triggered in Australia was exhilarating, traumatising, messy and uneven. It became not just a revolution against sexual violence, but a vector for long-awaited conversations about power: as it continued to dominate the media into 2018, responses to #MeToo fractured along the lines of race and privilege, and exposed longstanding schisms within feminism itself.

In a surprising twist, many heroes of the feminist old guard offered not solidarity, but opprobrium. Germaine Greer, in decadently crass form, typecast Weinstein's celebrity victims as "whingeing" too long after the fact. "If you spread your legs because he said 'be nice to me and I'll give you a job in a movie', then I'm afraid that's tantamount to consent," she told *The Sydney Morning Herald*, seemingly oblivious that actresses who did rebuff Weinstein's advances, as Mira Sorvino had, were subsequently blacklisted. For many feminists, old and young, #MeToo embodied a waifish brand of feminism. There was a clear nostalgia for the 1970s brand of plucky women who demanded their right to bodily autonomy, outwitted "foolish letches" and would have no qualms dead-eyeing a gropy guy with a firm retort.

In the eyes of the hundred French feminists who signed the "witch hunt" letter in *Le Monde*, and several younger high-profile feminists such as Katie Roiphe and Bari Weiss, #MeToo accusers and adherents had forfeited their power and agency. From this viewpoint, it seemed, "women could solve the problem of sexual harassment and assault with good humour, patience and a high tolerance for pain," wrote Moira Donegan in *The Guardian*.

What these surprising interventions exposed, according to Donegan, was a "serious intellectual rift" within feminism, which had:

> come to contain two distinct understandings of sexism, and two wildly different, often incompatible ideas of how that problem should be solved. One approach is individualist, hard-headed, grounded in ideals of pragmatism, realism and self-sufficiency. The other is expansive, communal, idealistic and premised on the ideals of mutual interest and solidarity.

This clash – restaged by #MeToo, but "decades in the making" – was essentially "a conflict between 'individualist' and 'social' feminisms." In part, Donegan wrote, this was a conflict over tactics: do we achieve the feminist project through "individual empowerment or through collective liberation"? More disturbing, perhaps, was "the moral divide between these two strands of thought" – where should the responsibility for sexual abuse be located? Was it "a woman's responsibility to navigate, withstand and overcome the misogyny that she encounters," or was it "the shared responsibility of all of us to eliminate sexism, so that she never encounters it in the first place"?

These were fractious debates, conducted in the mainstream press and through real-time stoushes on social media. It also brought the movement back to earth. In those early euphoric months, there were a lot of lofty claims made about the emancipatory power of #MeToo, and a tendency to universalise the experience of all women via a single experience: being subject to sexism, misogyny, coercion and abuse by men. That did promote some solidarity: the award-winning filmmaker Paromita Vohra described to the BBC, for example, how the testimonies of Indian women, in their granular detail, revealed previously unknown connections between rural and urban women. But ultimately – just like in India, where conversations about #MeToo inevitably led back to the perennial inequities of caste and class – a movement about the exploitation of power and privilege was bound to expose some of its own internal rifts and hypocrisies.

Here in Australia – where secrets and lies are still so tightly enmeshed with our national identity, and feminism has long stood in tension with the aims and objectives of minority groups – the criticisms surfaced quickly. Who was the #MeToo movement really for? As Dr Tess Ryan, an Aboriginal woman from Birpai country, wrote for *The Conversation*, "for many black women, the #MeToo movement requires a larger discussion about power imbalances in society … our fight goes deeper into the roots of colonial power to which we have never consented."

Other women felt betrayed as a certain kind of victim – generally young, able-bodied and white – received attention and support, while they were excluded. These reckonings were long overdue. They led to serious soul-searching among many non-Indigenous women about the true nature of inequality and privilege, and how the intersections of class, race, sexuality and disability would need to be foregrounded if the movement was going to go anywhere close to representing all women.

*

Across Australia, the impact of #MeToo was absorbed in ways that were intensely personal. All these things we'd been so scared to talk about had become, virtually overnight, a topic of casual conversation. There was something urgent about this – it was as though society had suddenly woken up, switched on the lights and seen the previously invisible mainframe of patriarchy. For the first time we could properly see clearly the house we didn't even know we'd been living in, with its trapdoors, dark hallways and secret stairwells. We could point to its design, identify its structural weaknesses – and maybe set about dismantling it. #MeToo worked like a skeleton key, exposing brutal realities and archaic social norms. Under this new and harsh light, things looked and felt very different.

Critically, it was not just women but men who were seeing the world anew. As brutal disclosures from friends and family filled their newsfeeds, men were genuinely shocked to learn that sexual harassment, assault and rape were not just commonplace, but part of the lived experience of virtually every woman they knew. "Until now, I thought I was awake," wrote journalist David Leser in the *Good Weekend*, "but the truth is I had absolutely no idea what women faced. No idea what it was like to feel afraid walking to my car, or jogging at night; to be pressed against on a crowded train; to be ignored or talked over repeatedly; to know that my value at work was often predicated on my sexual attractiveness to my boss. No idea what it was like to have someone indecently expose themselves to me; to have to devise strategies each day, often unconsciously, to just feel safe."

For women, what had so long remained unspoken and even unacknowledged was now on the surface.

"#MeToo changed my life," Lucia Osborne-Crowley tells me, from her apartment in London. Back in 2017, Osborne-Crowley was a reporter in Sydney, working in the burgeoning area of gendered violence. She reported frequently on the violence of men against women. But she was determined never to tell anyone what one man had done to her.

A decade earlier, when she was fifteen, Osborne-Crowley was raped at knifepoint by a man in a public bathroom. He was drunk, reeking of whisky and cigarettes, and as he assaulted her over and over she was sure she was about to die. Pressed against the cubicle door, she caught sight of a broken bottle on the floor, grabbed it and smashed it against the toilet bowl. Her attacker recoiled just enough for her to lunge for the door, unlock it, and run down three flights of stairs "as fast as my tiny, teenaged legs could carry me." She went home, washed away the blood and the evidence, and resolved to keep it a secret.

Just before #MeToo went viral, this story poured out of her for the first time. It was in private, with her therapist, and she never meant it to go any further. What would be the point of telling her friends? It would be a burden for them, and they would never truly understand. Besides, telling someone wouldn't change what had happened. "It just felt futile."

But then #MeToo happened. "My friends were all talking about it – not just what was happening publicly, but about what had happened in their own lives. It wasn't like other political conversations we'd had, because this was all about sharing things we had been ashamed of." Osborne-Crowley was astonished to find that almost every woman she knew had their own story of sexual harassment, assault or rape. She knew the statistics, knew that such violations were "prevalent." But this was a new kind of knowing.

"All of a sudden," says Osborne-Crowley, "people I respected were saying that talking about sexual assault was important politically. It made me feel like speaking about it could have benefits, rather than just being a drain on the people around me."

Nascent conversations about sexual harassment, assault and rape were happening spontaneously all over Australia. In my own family, the women closest to me disclosed terrible things they had never talked about. Often these stories would surface suddenly, in the middle of otherwise benign conversations, when we were out driving, at a café, after watching a movie. Like one of my close female relatives, who told me about the guy who held her over a balcony by her ankles when she was a little girl, and the bus driver who drove off route one night and took her to a cemetery. I heard, for the first time, stories about men in my own extended family who had been abusive, and had threatened to kill their wives. These were secrets that none of these women had ever thought to tell – until suddenly it became intolerable to keep them inside any longer. It made me reassess other stories I'd been told by women I loved, who were now long gone; stories I'd never thought to interrogate that now left unanswerable questions – like why did my grandmother drop the phone in fright that time her ex-husband called after years of no contact?

I counted myself lucky: I'd had close calls but had never been physically assaulted. And yet, as these conversations persisted, my own experience of sexual harassment became more vivid in my memory, and the anger I still felt about it harder to suppress.

In my mind's eye I see an expensive car with the roof down, and a 21-year-old in the passenger seat. Driving is my boss, silver-haired, more than old enough to be my father. Charismatic man, always up for a chat. Warm and friendly. Macquarie Street – old money, courts, parliament – slides by. He's made excuses to get me alone this afternoon. It's been weird for a while – sometimes he holds my hand when we're going to meetings, but I've always told myself it's in a "mates" kind of way. "I'm in love with you," he says suddenly. "When you first walked into my office, your breasts spoke to me." Sharp intake of breath – quiet, so he doesn't notice. Thoughts arrange like trained soldiers and fall quickly into line. *I don't want this.* But my discomfort is secondary. His comfort is primary. *Look after him first – you can wait.* I can't shame him. I'm the keeper of this secret now. "You don't really want me," I say, reaching for a reason he will accept, "and it's no good for you to go after younger women all the time. You need more than what they can give you." I'm counselling him now, keeping the keel even. He's persistent, but he's not an animal. We part ways back at work, until the next morning, when he calls me into his office again. "I've got a date tonight," he says, "and I want you to find us somewhere to eat." Like I'm his fucking personal assistant. I oblige, keeping it even. I sit across from him, looking for restaurants, and he smirks. What he says next I will play over and again in my mind for years: "This should keep the pressure off you for a while." The shame is mine now to own. Later, a colleague will tell me everyone at work thought I fucked the boss to get a promotion.

Seventeen years later, I have a cellular memory of that young woman who believed, truly believed, that she was just a person, like anybody else. Who didn't know that the sex she was born with had positioned her in the world as something other. Who hadn't thought much about feminism, because she didn't think she had to. As Gloria Steinem once said to an audience member despairing over her niece's lack of interest in feminism: "Don't worry – life will radicalise her."

Mine is not a horror story. It's ordinary. I don't tell it to foreground my experience or because I need to unburden myself. I tell it to get inside that mechanism of secret-keeping. The deep knowing in so many women that when men express their entitlement to treat you as a sexual object you must conceal the shamefulness of their actions, both from the public eye and from them. We protect them from the sting of humiliation, ultimately, in order to protect ourselves. Women know in their bones that a humiliated man can be a dangerous one. A powerful one, even more so. We shame them at our peril.

But the practice of secret-keeping is not just about keeping men's secrets from the wider world; it can also be about keeping those secrets from ourselves – burying them deep inside, where we can try to forget them altogether.

One woman I spoke to discovered how this secret-keeping was affecting her own life, and that of the girls she grew up with. On their street had lived a paedophile – a white man who ingratiated himself with the largely Indigenous community – who had abused her and several of her friends. "And he was still out there, just living his life in Sydney," she says. Despite remaining close as they grew older, none of them had ever talked about it. In fact, they still saw him occasionally – just five years earlier, on a trip to Sydney to go to a concert, they had even stayed at his house. "I think that just speaks volumes about this man and what he had done to all these young Aboriginal women," she says, "and how we had kind of accepted it. It just become a part of our lives. Because you don't want to ruffle feathers. And why would you want to speak out?" One weekend in 2019, she and eight of her childhood friends – with thirty-five children and two grandchildren between them – went on a weekend away together. For the first time, they talked about what this paedophile had done to them, and how it had affected them. Everyone had grown up around some kind of abuse, and many were living then with abusive partners. But that weekend was "a big turning point for us, as a group of women," she says. "We made some commitments around healing, and around identifying these men. We made a decision that we would support each other, no matter what."

*

What was particularly remarkable about those early, heady months of #MeToo was that every new allegation against a high-profile man opened up a new frontier for conversation and debate. If you believed Dylan Farrow's allegations of childhood sexual abuse against Woody Allen, could you still enjoy his movies? Could you "love the art, but deplore the artist"? When Louis CK admitted the allegations of sexual misconduct against him were true, and apologised, we argued over whether an apology like this – one that sounded so thoughtful and contrite – should absolve someone who had done such harm.

But of all these debates, none was so divisive – or as revealing – as the one that raged over the controversial outing of comedian Aziz Ansari. Depending on whom you spoke to, it was either a necessary reckoning with the ubiquitous harm of sexual coercion and disrespect, or the moment #MeToo jumped the shark and went too far, threatening to derail the movement altogether.

In the heat of the moment, these divisions seemed deep and unresolvable. I don't intend to re-prosecute the many debates that followed, but I do think it was a breakthrough moment for #MeToo. For people open to it, this was a crucial phase of the awakening – both for women who'd become resigned to the "normality" of men's sexual coercion, but more importantly for some men, who'd never imagined that this could do such harm. These men were prompted to interrogate their own sexual practices precisely because Ansari was *not* a monster. He was, in many ways, just like them. And yet he had caused this woman such distress that she had, rightly or wrongly, felt she had been *assaulted*.

The Aziz Ansari story broke right at the height of #MeToo, on 13 January 2018. On the website Babe.net – aimed at "girls who don't give a fuck" – was a detailed account by "Grace," an anonymous 23-year-old photographer, of a sexual encounter she had with Ansari, which she described as "by far the worst experience with a man I've ever had."

I'm going to detail this story so there's no ambiguity about what happened. The two met at the Emmys after-party, and later went on a dinner date before returning to Ansari's apartment. Everything started out fine: they were kissing, but things were escalating quickly – he was undressing her, then himself, and then he told her he was going to grab a condom. Grace wanted to put the brakes on, and said something like, "Whoa, let's relax for a sec, let's chill." At first, Ansari seemed to understand; then he went down on her and asked her to do the same, which she agreed to. Grace said that afterwards Ansari kept moving her hand towards his penis throughout the night, even after she kept moving her hand away. It became a cat-and-mouse routine; she would get up and move away from him, he would follow her and repeat the crude move of sticking his fingers down her throat, and then down her pants. "It felt like a fucking game," Grace said. She kept giving Ansari strong hints about how uncomfortable she was – pulling away, mumbling, even going completely still. When he kept asking "again and again" where she wanted him to fuck her, she evaded him, until saying "next time," at which point Ansari offered her a drink and asked if that would count as a second date. When he poured her a glass, she excused herself to go to the bathroom so she could clear her head. When she returned, Ansari asked if she was okay, and Grace replied: "I don't want to feel forced, because then I'll hate you, and I'd rather not hate you." His reaction was textbook sensitivity: "Oh of course," he replied, "it's only fun if we're both having fun," and then asked her to chill on the couch. She sat on the floor next to Ansari, who was on the couch, and thought "he might rub [my] back or play with [my] hair – something to calm [me] down." Instead, he instructed her to turn around, then sat back and pointed to his penis, motioning for her to go down on him. She did, but only because she felt pressured. When he pulled her back onto the couch, he kissed her again and said, "Doesn't look like you hate me." Then – and this was despite Grace being clear several times by then that she did not want to have sex with him – Ansari brought over a large mirror, bent her over and started ramming his penis against her ass, asking, "Where do you want me to fuck you? Do you want me to fuck you right here?" Grace stood up and said, "No, I don't think I'm ready to do this, I really don't think I'm going to do this," at which point Ansari finally relented, and suggested they "just chill, but this time with our clothes on." They went to the couch, and he turned on an episode of *Seinfeld*. As she sat there, Grace was reeling – she felt "violated" and "emotional." As this was sinking in, Ansari kissed her, and again stuck his fingers down her throat and moved to undo her pants. She turned away, and her resolve hardened. "You guys are all the same, you guys are all the fucking same." Ansari asked her what she meant, and when she turned to answer he met her with "gross forceful kisses." When Grace moved away and said she was calling a car, he hugged her, kissed her "aggressively," and then when she pulled away, he insisted that he would call her a car instead. Grace cried the whole ride home.

The response to this story was visceral and immediate. Here's the conundrum: it depicted a situation that was both horrible and yet "so banal that calling it sexual assault" would render sexual assault "omnipresent." Of course, invoking the specific legal term "assault" drew a lot of heat: not least because it significantly upped the stakes for Ansari, who clearly (and, many would say, correctly) believed the encounter was consensual. We know from the text messages exchanged after that night that Ansari was "surprised and concerned" to learn that Grace was so upset. "All I can say is, it would never be my intention to make you or anyone feel the way you described," he texted her. "Clearly, I misread things in the moment and I'm truly sorry."

Ansari had many defenders, and there was little support for the notion that he had committed sexual assault. But one of the reasons this story resonated so strongly – with women and men – was because there was such vehement disagreement. As the feminist writer Jessica Valenti tweeted, "A lot of men will read that post about Aziz Ansari and see an everyday, reasonable sexual interaction. But part of what women are saying right now is that what the culture considers 'normal' sexual encounters are not working for us, and oftentimes [are] harmful." The most important – and culture-changing – question that arose was: How could one person's consensual encounter be another's sexual trauma?

"I think a lot of people read that and thought, 'I've been in that situation, and I never felt like I had permission to talk about how it affected me,'" says Osborne-Crowley. "Similarly, I think it caused a lot of men to reflect; 'What are some nights in my history that could be this exact story?'"

She's right. For the men willing to see past their own defensiveness, the Ansari story was a terrifying wake-up call. Writing for *Vox*, one anonymous male writer said the scenario was horrifyingly familiar. Reflecting on one encounter – in which he had coerced, pestered and tried to manipulate his friend into having sex – he wrote: "I'm still not sure what to call what I did – assault? Coercion? A violation? What I do believe is this: If I hadn't stopped when I stopped, I would have committed rape. But in that moment, it didn't feel that way – it felt normal. I had convinced myself that she still wanted me despite her objections." This was how he – like so many men – had been socialised. He'd had his first orgasm to porn, "where consent to have sex is implicit." Men, he wrote, were taught young that sex was about "conquest, competition, and a measure of self-worth." There was rarely any punishment for pressuring a woman into sex; only "the reward of sexual pleasure if we succeed." Not to mention the status. Essentially, a lot of men approached sex like an '80s salesman: never take no for an answer, and always be closing.

It was clear to this anonymous writer that men had been ignoring all the ways in which women say no, and that needed to stop. "We need to make 'enthusiastic consent' our mantra ... Men, especially the most liberal, caring, and self-aware among us: look harder at yourselves. Rape culture ends when we stop raping."

Toby, a product designer living in Sydney, had exactly the same nauseating realisation. Speaking on the UTS podcast "After #MeToo," he said that #MeToo had revealed to him and his close male friends that their whole idea of consent was "wrong." "You probably did sexually harass or, you know, assault girls in hindsight … by coercing or being persistent," he said. In reflecting on his own sexual history, there were "lots of moments" that made him think, "Jesus, that was really horrible of me to do that." These banal encounters were now something he questioned: "I can't believe I did that." He recalled an ordinary scene – repeatedly trying to go further with a girl he was kissing, even when she pushed his hand away several times. "I think that would have made her feel really uncomfortable," he said, quietly. "If you get told 'no' in any form – whether it's an action or a word – that's a no. She probably had less trust for me after that as well, so you know … that's horrible."

In one of many conversations Toby had about the definition of consent, he recalled one with a close male friend when it "dawned on us that shit … we've gone past consent." Instead of just feeling bad about that and changing the subject, they kept talking about how horrible and guilty they felt; and how they needed to talk about consent with their friends. Before #MeToo, he said, subjects like consent and sexual assault were almost never talked about in his friendship circles. "I think before #MeToo, there was that doubt … *are they telling the truth?* Innocent until proven guilty, sort of thing. After #MeToo that changed completely. Now I realise how rampant it is."

In 2019, performing to 200 people in New York, Ansari talked for the first time about how the story affected his life. "It's a terrifying thing to talk about," he told the audience. "There were times I felt really upset and humiliated and embarrassed, and ultimately I just felt terrible this person felt this way. But you know, after a year, how I feel about it is, I hope it was a step forward. It made me think about a lot, and I hope I've become a better person." Ansari related a conversation he had with a friend, who'd said the story had made him reassess the way he'd been with women. "If that has made not just me but other guys think about this," Ansari said, "that's a good thing."

Ultimately, if #MeToo was going to come close to a real examination of power, it had to be dragged out of the boardroom, off the casting couch and into the bedrooms of ordinary people. The Ansari story got people closer into those grey areas that we need to interrogate – can we situate bad and unwanted sex on the spectrum of behaviours that eventually lead to assault and rape? And how can we change the way men are socialised, so that sexual coercion and disrespect are no longer the norm? And can we get the balance right between freedom and accountability?

*

The various storylines emerging from #MeToo kept returning us to a fundamental set of questions: Who gets to tell men's secrets? Whose secrets are we ready to hear? Which secrets are *proper* to tell in public, and how? What is the cost of telling them? What should happen once the truth is known?

In Australia, a disturbing trend emerged in the twelve months following #MeToo: most of the women whose stories went public did not give their consent. Eryn Jean Norvill, as we've seen, made her complaint internally, never wanted it to be published, but then felt obliged to join a high-stakes defamation trial that lasted months and threatened to derail her career.

Then there was Catherine Marriott, the rural advocate and businesswoman who, after agonising over the decision for two years, finally worked up the courage to report Barnaby Joyce to the West Australian branch of the National Party for sexual misconduct; her complaint was also leaked to the press, presumably by Joyce's political enemies.

Then came Ashleigh Raper, the ABC journalist who reported the then leader of the NSW Labor Party, Luke Foley, for putting his hand inside her underpants at a Christmas party; her allegation was revealed under parliamentary privilege by one of Foley's political rivals, the then corrections minister, Liberal MP David Elliot. Unlike #MeToo stories in the United States, which were often characterised by careful reporting, many of Australia's most high-profile #MeToo stories represented yet another violation of the woman's consent.

The price these women paid for being named was profound. Marriott said that having her name leaked was "one of the most frightening things you will ever have to live through ... you finally find the courage within yourself to stand up for what you believe in and then all control is taken away." When she discovered that journalists had her name, she was "a shell. I couldn't move, I couldn't speak. It was awful. My phone went feral and I just turned it off." Joyce denied the allegations, and an internal National Party inquiry into them was "inconclusive."

Even after Foley called Raper to apologise for being a "drunk idiot," he subsequently denied the allegations, and announced he was suing her for defamation (before dropping his claim a few weeks later). Raper had kept quiet because she feared both losing her position as a state political reporter and the negative impact the publicity would have on her and her young family. "This impact is now being felt profoundly," she said in a statement. "Situations like mine should not be discussed in parliament for the sake of political point scoring."

#MeToo may have shifted the world on its axis, but in Australia many of the old rules remained intact. Yes, the media now had an appetite for outing high-profile predators, and yes, their female accusers were increasingly being given the benefit of the doubt. But a forcefield of resistance still ringed the old boys' clubs, and their willingness to exact archaic forms of public retribution went largely unchecked. Any woman with the gall to reveal one of their secrets would be reminded that exposing a powerful "mate" would still cost her a pound of her flesh.

That cost was extracted from Tessa Sullivan in January 2018. Having just resigned from her job as a councillor at Melbourne City Council, she picked up the *Herald Sun* and found herself and her son, his face blurred, on the front page. As she stared in disbelief, her son recognised his swimsuit and exclaimed, "Look, Mum – that's me!" The photo had been taken by her husband: a sweet image of Sullivan at the beach in her bikini, embracing her little boy. Emblazoned over it, in huge white block letters, was the headline: ROB, I'M SO LUCKY TO HAVE YOU.

"Rob" was Robert Doyle, then Lord Mayor of Melbourne, whom Sullivan had, just days earlier, reported for sexual harassment and indecent assault. Her complaint had been internal, and was leaked to the media without her consent. Her 24-page complaint to the council was written in excruciating detail – the kind of statement police prepare before a trial – and was accompanied by a statement from fellow councillor Dr Cathy Oke, who was also alleging sexual harassment. So serious were these allegations, the Melbourne City Council appointed a renowned Melbourne silk, Ian Freckelton, to investigate them. In the *Herald Sun*'s front-page story, however, there was no mention of Oke – just a clear depiction of Sullivan as a jilted woman who "wouldn't take no for an answer." The evidence? Text messages Sullivan had sent to colleagues at the council; the bikini shot sent as a joke to colleagues stuck in the office while she was on holiday. In one, she calls Doyle "darl," and in another, she thanked him for his support. As far as *Herald Sun* readers knew, however, these texts were intimate exchanges between Doyle and Sullivan.

This was a surgical strike against Sullivan. It's unclear how the *Herald Sun* got the texts and photos: *The Age* said they'd been provided by the PR company hired by Doyle, while Stephen Mayne at *Crikey* reported they were sought out by the *Herald Sun* after Doyle gave evidence to the Freckelton inquiry. Says Sullivan, "The [*Herald Sun*] behaved appallingly unethically. Like, they didn't even bother to ring to check anything," she says. The *Herald Sun* would publish another article implying that Sullivan was so obsessed with Doyle she had even changed her name. "My actual maiden name is Doyle," she says with still-potent fury, "which was actually printed in their paper *twice* when my grandparents died ... so you could just Google it." As a lawyer, Sullivan knew she could sue the paper. But for what? "I could take five years out of my life. I've got the money; I can do that. But I was literally like, 'What, so that they can write an apology on page 30 in font nine?'"

Journalistic accuracy was never the point. As former Melbourne City councillor Stephen Mayne wrote in *Crikey*, the *Herald Sun* launched this full-scale attack on Sullivan because Doyle had old mates there; they had "dined together many times over the years." This was a classic case of powerful mates closing ranks: slut-shame the accusing harridan, reverse victim and offender and give her a "motive." The same old playbook, but from a now bygone era. In the four short months since #MeToo went viral, what may have looked like just another sleazy tabloid story was seen for what it had always been: a blatantly egregious attempt to discredit a woman in order to protect a powerful man.

What made the *Herald Sun*'s brazen victim-blaming even more nauseating was that Sullivan's allegations against the Lord Mayor were serious: sustained sexual harassment, and an indecent assault so forceful it bruised her chest. One night, he lunged at her in the back seat of a car; Sullivan, terrified, "slapped the hell out of him." Another night, following her to the lift after Town Hall was closed, Doyle made a blunt sexual reference to "going down" in the lift together, exclaiming "I love cunnilingus!" He then insisted, despite Sullivan's repeated refusals, that she get a lift home with him. In the carpark, as she attempted to leave, she felt corralled into the back seat by Doyle and his driver. When Sullivan again insisted she wanted to get out and walk, Doyle refused. Sullivan waited until the driver stopped at a give-way sign, opened the car door and bolted. By then she was being subjected to daily acts of inappropriate touching and humiliations in team meetings, in which Doyle would beckon her to kneel beside him so he could show her some documents, and then, in a room full of people, look down her top. "It was getting to the point where it was ludicrous: he was following me from meeting to meeting. It was so bad." She tried to change the way she dressed and behaved, thinking that might restrain him. "I'd dress more conservative, or say, 'No, I'm not going to get a lift off you,' or make sure I was never alone with him, thinking it's always on me; when really, this person is a total predator."

Doyle's sexual predation was an open secret at Town Hall, the culture recalling that around Harvey Weinstein. New female councillors were warned never to go to meetings alone with Doyle or accept lifts home with him late at night. Says Sullivan, "Councillors would sit between me and him because they knew what he was like." When she submitted her resignation along with her detailed statement just before Christmas in 2017, management urged her to reconsider. "They were like, 'Oh, we know all about it. Why don't we just rip up your resignation paper?' Like, *don't even worry about it — we'll handle it, he's always like this.*"

In fact, Doyle's lechery was well known. As prominent ABC Melbourne radio broadcaster Jon Faine would later admit, Doyle's penchant for "pretty young colleagues was notorious public knowledge within a circle of important and influential people." These weren't just rumours; Doyle's "undue attention" towards some of the young women who worked with Faine went far enough to cause "some embarrassment." "We always thought that he was just a bit lecherous," said Faine. "But it is quite clear that Robert Doyle's behaviour has gone far beyond that … If I'm part of the problem for never having brought it to anyone's attention, then I regret that and I apologise." Melbourne author Helen Garner — who has herself, since *The First Stone*, felt the ire reserved for those who defend powerful men accused of sexual harassment — had no sympathy for Faine's position. In a letter to *The Age*, she wrote:

> It seems a bit late for Faine to come over righteous now, while the debris from the explosion rains down all over the city. Did he tell Mr Doyle: 'The way you behave around women is distressing to them and embarrassing to all of us. The women hate it. This is their workplace. You're the lord mayor, for God's sake. It's time you noticed the effect of your behaviour on other people'. Perhaps we can start asking ourselves how and why some men's sleazy behaviour patterns are left free to develop past the point of tolerability.

If Doyle's behaviour was notorious among Melbourne's "important and influential people," apparently someone forgot to tell former Victorian premier Jeff Kennett and 3AW's Neil Mitchell, who claimed that Doyle had been subject to "a lynch mob mentality." By 5 February 2018, four women had come forward with reports of sexual harassment and misconduct dating back to 1997, and *The Age* had reported that at least three more had contacted the Freckleton investigation with allegations of inappropriate behaviour spanning Doyle's career, back to when he was a schoolteacher at Geelong College. Nonetheless, Kennett, sticking by his mate, declared the mounting allegations a "political witch-hunt." Doyle was, said Kennett, "a very likeable individual" and "not a predator" (as though #MeToo had not already destroyed the idea that such attributes were mutually exclusive). Besides, he went on: "[it] takes two to tango ... [s]ome of the claims are very light ... [t]here's been no sexual attacks in terms of the more serious forms of sexual activity. It's about a hand on the knee, a kiss, a pat on the back and the more substantial claim by the ex-councillor."

But in the #MeToo era, life comes at you fast. Within a week, claims against Doyle by two former students were being investigated by Victoria Police, and other former students had come forward, including one former schoolgirl who said Doyle, while giving her a lift back from sport one day, had repeatedly "mistook" the gear stick for her thighs. Another woman accused Doyle of assaulting her at two separate Liberal Party functions. By 11 February, Kennett recanted somewhat, telling the Herald Sun he felt "let down" by Doyle's misconduct.

"You see these power constructs," Sullivan says. "Like, how did Weinstein get away with it for so long? How did Bill Cosby, how did Jimmy Savile? How? Because these people around them accepted this behaviour in a way — they normalised it. And they protected them.

"Robert Doyle was out there grabbing all his mates to just bag me, bag me, bag me, knowing that because we were in litigation I couldn't comment publicly," she says. The impact on Sullivan and her family was severe: at the height of it, they were getting up to fifty calls a day from journalists, and even had to move house to evade the constant harassment. "They were brutal," she says. "We're just freaking civilians — we have no idea how to handle stuff. I lost seventeen kilos in three months. I couldn't even walk my kids to school on their first day. I was so depressed about the whole thing."

If Doyle had limited his predation to a small group of women, the Herald Sun's tactics may have succeeded in shutting down the story. Sullivan says she was contacted by several other women who had been considering coming forward but changed their minds after seeing what they did to her. "They'd tell me, *Oh my God, I'm never ever coming forward,*" she says. "*That's gonna happen to me. I'm going to be slut-shamed. Are you kidding me? No way.*"

Throughout this experience, the only thing that kept Sullivan going was the knowledge that she had something no one else had – "not the Herald Sun, not Jeff Kennett, not Robert Doyle." "What I have is the truth. I just kept thinking, 'That's got to come out, it will come out. I just know it.'"

It did. Even though "dozens" have contacted Sullivan with stories about Doyle they'll never make public, the sheer volume of his offending was such that even the tip of that iceberg was enough to sink him. By March 2018, the City of Melbourne inquiry had upheld Sullivan's and Oke's claims, and council CEO Ben Rimmer summarised its findings by saying the workplace had not been safe for either of them. He said Sullivan had, in being the first to speak out, taken a "very significant and courageous personal step." Doyle – whose legal fees for the inquiry were paid for by the City of Melbourne, "because," Sullivan explains, "as Lord Mayor, he was insured" – responded to the findings via a statement from his wife, Emma Page-Campbell. The allegations were untrue, he maintained; simply "misunderstandings" caused by his "cheerful" and "sometimes animated" manner, which he recognised "may no longer be appropriate by today's standards." Stephen Mayne, who had witnessed Doyle touching councillor Cathy Oke's thighs repeatedly at a public dinner, called for Doyle's Companion of the Order of Australia – the highest award in Australia's honour system – to be revoked. "Sexual predators shouldn't keep their gongs," Mayne wrote in Crikey, "but don't expect to hear that line from the long-serving men who run Melbourne."

There was never anything in this for Sullivan. All she wanted was for Doyle never again to occupy a position from which he could harass or assault someone subordinate to him. "None of us have ever received a cent, nor do we want that," she says. "That was one thing that I remember the investigators saying to me: 'We can't figure out what motive you have. If you did this for a political reason, it's like career suicide. You obviously haven't done this for money – you're wealthy and haven't asked for anything.' The main reason why they really believed me, I think, was because there was no agenda."

Ultimately, though, aside from securing Doyle's resignation, she's not sure what she achieved. Sullivan had come to politics after years of living with an autoimmune disease so severe she had to use a wheelchair and had hoped to make a difference in the disability sector. Within two years of joining Melbourne City Council, she had not only been sexually harassed and indecently assaulted, but had lost her political career, been publicly shamed and would now be forever associated with the man who harassed and assaulted her. "Any job you go for, the first thing someone's gonna do is google you – and I hate the fact that I'm always next to my perpetrator. That's not the legacy I wanted to leave," she says. "I don't want to be some #MeToo person. It just annoys me that when you're known for something like this, people think that's what you wanted … Nobody goes, 'Oh good, I've been sexually harassed – I'm gonna go and be the face of something.'"

For Sullivan, the process of being Australia's first political #MeToo case was not only brutalising, but dehumanising. "I had all that innocence, that greatness and purity and positivity about life and career, and that's just so damaged now … But at the same time, all the pain that I went through," she says, equivocating, "I feel like I can help other women. It's a strange place to be in … I'll never really feel good about it, you know?"

As we finish our phone call, I find myself needing to reassure Sullivan that what she did really has been meaningful. Here was a woman who, after being raised by a single mother in Thailand, had taken on one of the most powerful men in Melbourne and was now studying journalism at Harvard. I tell her she has made an impact, and the way she has carried herself has been exemplary.

I think Tessa Sullivan knows all of this intellectually, but I wonder if she'll ever truly believe it.

TURNBULL > MORRISON

> I had to do something – I had no excuse. If you have political capital, you can be certain of one thing: it will disappear. You don't keep political capital for very long and you either see it disappear through inaction, or you spend it on a good cause.
>
> —John Howard

In the wake of the Port Arthur massacre in 1996, newly elected prime minister John Howard made a quick, bold decision. Within twelve days he had outflanked the mighty gun lobby and, in the face of furious opposition, introduced radical gun-control laws.

The shock of Port Arthur created the political capital, and Howard had the courage to burn it. His "blanket law" would catch "the innocent and the responsible as well as the venal," he told SBS's *Insight*, but Howard was willing to be indiscriminate. "There was a price, but in the national interest, a price worth paying."

Culture shocks are often a necessary precondition for systemic change. In 2017, #MeToo had exposed archaic social norms and it had endowed women, whose claims had for centuries been reflexively disbelieved, with the benefit of the doubt. The fury, shock and disbelief of #MeToo had generated a pile of political capital. But would the government have the courage – or the will – to spend it?

The spring conditions in Canberra that year were atypical: Australia had a conservative government led by an openly feminist prime minister. Malcolm Turnbull, an unlikely Liberal in more ways than one, hadn't merely jumped on a popular bandwagon – he'd nailed his feminist colours to the mast back in 1988, when the conservative backlash against feminism was at its peak. "I think I am, and most people regard me as very much, a feminist," he said in a televised interview. "I've never preferred all-male company to mixed company. I like working with women very much. A lot of men are very uncomfortable with women in equal positions in business and I've never had that problem." By 2017 – when third-wave feminism had been cresting for years – Turnbull was still a Coalition outlier, even among his senior female ministers: Julie Bishop and Michaelia Cash (the latter of whom was minister for women) steadfastly refused to call themselves feminists.

In 2015, when Turnbull ousted Tony Abbott – as prime minister *and* minister for women – he wanted to send a signal: gender equality was high on his agenda. Seizing the momentum generated by Australian of the Year Batty, Turnbull made it his first order of business to pledge $100 million to domestic violence prevention. It wasn't the money that mattered; it wasn't nearly enough, anyway, and the package was planned under Abbott. What mattered was the way Turnbull delivered it – and that he meant what he said. In a statement he would return to many times, Turnbull paraphrased his wife, former Sydney lord mayor and Our Watch ambassador Lucy Turnbull: "Disrespecting women does not always result in violence against women. But all violence against women begins with disrespecting women." The message was clear: Australia's new prime minister was rejecting the anachronistic sexism of his predecessor. "It is my dream," Turnbull said, "that Australia will in the future be known for respecting women."

So starved were we of modern leadership that even his acknowledgment of gender inequality, and how that manifested in disrespect and violence towards women, was heralded as a breakthrough. "We finally are starting to hear from the leaders of our country that they are addressing this issue, that they recognise the responsibility they have to lead our society, our communities, by speaking the language we need to hear," said a clearly relieved Batty.

By 2017, it was clear to most sentient Australians that Turnbull's dream to render disrespect for women "un-Australian" would require *a lot* of work. In late September 2017, three weeks before #MeToo, Turnbull was approached with some "uniquely awkward" news. The Australian federal police were "concerned" that Nationals MP George Christensen had for three years been spending more than 100 days a year outside Australia – most of it in the Philippines, staying in "seedy hotels" in Manila's red-light areas. An investigation would later find no evidence of illegality, although police inquiries were hindered by "encrypted messages." Christensen maintains he was visiting his fiancée (whom he's since married), despite only meeting her in 2017, after he'd already travelled to the Philippines nineteen times. Nevertheless, in late 2017, Turnbull knew for certain that the Nationals had an MP who was spending a third of the year in an area notorious for Australian men engaging in sex tourism, and nobody in the Nationals seemed to know, or care. As he recalled in his memoir, "The hypocrisy made me sick."

That same year, as *Four Corners* would reveal in 2020, he would be forced to pull aside Christian Porter, then minister for social services, and give him a stern warning: as a married man with a small child, it was not just inappropriate for him to be getting drunk and intimate with young female staffers in Canberra bars; it could leave him vulnerable to compromise or blackmail from foreign agents.

By February 2018, Turnbull was fighting fires on several fronts. After receiving an "unequivocal assurance" from his deputy prime minister, Barnaby Joyce, that rumours about him having an affair with his staffer were false, Turnbull learnt through the *Daily Telegraph* that not only was Joyce in a sexual relationship with Vicki Campion but that they were expecting a baby. Turnbull responded by announcing a revision to the ministerial code of conduct that would prohibit ministers from having sex with their staffers. "I don't care whether they are married or single, I don't care," he said, sounding like a frustrated parent. In corporate Australia, where Turnbull had spent most of his career, having sex with your staff was as much of a relic as the long lunch.

The problem, as Turnbull saw it, was not just that ministers might be having sex with their staffers; it was that they didn't see anything wrong with it. There was almost no comprehension, it seemed, of the power dynamics that underpin sexual harassment and abuse in the workplace.

For his attempt to drag Canberra into the modern world, Turnbull received support from only two cabinet ministers: Scott Morrison and Christopher Pyne. But his future minister for women, Kelly O'Dwyer, was clear in her approval, saying, "The idea that the code has created a new licence for intrusion into politicians' lives is a nonsense."

Within days of the "bonk ban," Joyce resigned as Nationals leader after Catherine Marriott's private complaint of sexual misconduct against him was leaked to the press.

Turnbull just couldn't catch a break. Before the week was out, former minister for women Michaelia Cash was forced to withdraw "disgraceful and sexist" comments about Bill Shorten's staffers, after she threatened in Senate Estimates to name "every young woman in Bill Shorten's office" about whom "rumours abound."

To put it mildly, Turnbull's vision to lead Australia towards a gender-equal future was not going according to plan. Behind these grisly scenes, however, there *was* work being done. Quietly, two ministers within the Turnbull government were preparing announcements that had the potential to radically reshape Australia's response to sexual violence and harassment in two key areas: universities and workplaces.

*

Turnbull wasn't the Coalition's only feminist. His new minister for women, Kelly O'Dwyer, not only had "no hesitation in identifying strongly as a feminist," but, as Georgie Dent observed in *Women's Agenda*, seemed "genuinely disinterested in accepting the status quo for women." She was already an exemplar of this: as the first cabinet minister to give birth while in office not just once but twice, she kept her position while her husband became primary carer for their children. O'Dwyer had also created a "fighting fund" to get more Liberal women elected, contributing $50,000 of her own money.

When O'Dwyer replaced Cash in December 2017, she had a singular opportunity – as minister for women and with a senior finance portfolio as minister for revenue and financial services. It was a powerful combination, but one that might not last: with an election likely in twelve months, she would have to work fast and be focused to achieve anything substantial.

When she met with sex discrimination commissioner Kate Jenkins. O'Dwyer was already contemplating where she should put her energy as minister for women. Given her finance background, she was considering what she could do to advance women's economic security. Jenkins also had an ambitious idea in mind. "I said, we've got the survey [on sexual harassment in Australia, which would report in September 2018]. The Commission has powers to conduct a national inquiry on workplace sexual harassment, and we could focus on solutions – it would be world-leading." Since the Weinstein story had broken, Jenkins had been asked to comment regularly on the issue of sexual harassment. "I had spent thirty years working on workplace sexual harassment, and I knew: this moment is different." As Jenkins saw it, the #MeToo movement had finally turned the tide: for the first time, Australia was having "a serious conversation about sexual harassment" and there was "an unprecedented appetite for solutions."

Talking to me over Zoom, Jenkins is palpably excited. "Can I take you on this journey?" she asks. It's clear she's thought about exactly what Quarterly Essay readers want to know about this moment, and her conviction is contagious.

As an employment lawyer through the 1990s and early 2000s, Jenkins witnessed firsthand how employers responded to the new laws against sexual harassment. The visionary Labor senator Susan Ryan had ensured sexual harassment was made illegal under the *Sex Discrimination Act 1984*, making this otherwise entirely normalised behaviour an issue employers had to deal with. In 1993, freshly graduated, Jenkins landed a job at a big corporate law firm, Freehill, Hollingdale and Page (now Herbert Smith Freehills), and within two years was put in charge of its equal opportunity practice. Jenkins became partner "in no time, because all these corporates needed help dealing with sexual harassment complaints, and none of the boys wanted to do it." Back then, employers needed to show they were taking steps to prevent harassment – policies, training – and if a complaint was substantiated, the awards were paltry: around $5000 to $10,000 ("the legals were $50k"). "So the economics – and the power dynamic – meant that really, people didn't bring cases, even if they wanted to."

In the 2000s, that calculation changed. Victims' lawyers, knowing that payouts would be nominal, started going to the media to leverage better deals for their clients. Prosecuted in the media, these matters could seriously damage reputations, and even affect share prices. Of this trend, the Kristy Fraser-Kirk story is emblematic: in 2010, after complaining that company director Mark McInnes had made unwanted sexual advances at company functions, she sued David Jones, McInnes and the company directors for $37 million – Australia's biggest-ever harassment claim. Eventually, the case was settled for $850,000, but the fallout was substantial: the story ran in the press for five months, and McInnes was forced to resign (albeit with a $1.5-million settlement). The blowback on Fraser-Kirk was savage – there's no question she paid by far the biggest price reputationally. But it put the wind up corporate Australia, and precipitated the rise of non-disclosure agreements. "Companies knew they'd have to settle, even if they didn't believe [the complaint] was true, because they couldn't afford the reputational damage," says Jenkins. They weren't paying compensation for not protecting staff. The employers were buying silence." Jenkins herself negotiated hundreds of disputes that ended up with NDAs. This didn't just gag victims from speaking publicly; in many cases, even senior management weren't made aware of settlements reached inside their own companies, because they were handled quickly and quietly by legal or HR. Don't ask, don't tell, don't look – don't worry. It forced the issue of sexual harassment even further underground, making it almost invisible. Jenkins recalls, after the Weinstein story broke, seeing numerous light-bulb moments at dinner parties. "All these men were saying, 'That sort of thing doesn't happen here,' and all the women were saying, 'What are you talking about?!'"

Sexual harassment – which was still considered normal and largely unavoidable in 2017 – was also widespread. Figures from the early 2010s put the rate of sexual harassment as high as one in five workers harassed in the previous five years – updated survey results in 2018 would find that had jumped to a stunning one in three.

In June 2018, Kelly O'Dwyer seized the moment and announced the launch of a national inquiry into sexual harassment, headed by Jenkins. "We can't find any other country that's looking at this issue in such a comprehensive manner," she said. What would become known as the Respect@ Work inquiry had a broad remit: to consider what causes sexual harassment in the workplace, the use of technology and social media, and the adequacy of existing laws. To "raised eyebrows" in her party room, O'Dwyer managed to secure $500,000 in federal funding for the twelve-month inquiry. Her ambition was clear. O'Dwyer didn't want to just "admire the problem" – she wanted to know how to solve it.

By June 2018, O'Dwyer wasn't the only Coalition minister ready to use the political capital created by #MeToo. Fellow moderate Simon Birmingham, then minister for education, was preparing to announce a taskforce that would oversee how Australian universities responded to complaints of sexual harassment and assault. The story that leads to that moment is complex, but reveals the necessity of Birmingham's initiative – and how tragic it was that it never saw the light of day.

*

#MeToo did not bring the crisis of rape and sexual harassment on campus to the nation's attention. In fact, it was the other way round: it was the dogged advocacy of students that contributed much of the heat to the eventual firestorm of #MeToo. For Sharna Bremner, the founder of End Rape on Campus Australia, this is a source of enormous frustration. "In my mind, students got us to where we are today," she tells me. "Students have been the ones fighting this fight for years, and nobody was listening. Before #MeToo, they were pounding the pavement, dragging mattresses around campuses and doing everything they could to get somebody to listen, and nobody cared," she says. When Bremner says this student activism predates

#MeToo, she's talking about a tradition that goes way back. "We found articles about activism dating back to the '40s and '50s."

The first national student survey, conducted by the Australian Human Rights Commission, was released in 2017. It found that in 2015 and 2016, 1.6 per cent of students had been sexually assaulted in a university setting. Even so, there was still an "incredible amount of resistance across the higher education sector to even recognise that sexual assault was an issue," says Bremner. "I had the deputy vice-chancellor of the University of Adelaide tell me that 'Sexual assault doesn't happen here.' I said, 'Then we need to call the UN, because you've found the one place on earth it doesn't happen, and we need to find out what the magic formula is.'"

For student survivors of sexual assault seeking redress, universities fall in a no-man's land between schools and workplaces. Unlike kids in high school, they're not covered by child protection laws; and unlike employees, they're not covered by workplace health and safety laws. (Employees raped in the workplace can make a civil claim and have vastly higher chances of getting some redress in the civil system than in the criminal courts.) "It's frustrating to see people continually put forward a broken system as the only answer," says Bremner. The required response, as she sees it, is clear: sexual assault is both an administrative *and* a criminal matter. Bremmer believes that unlike children and employees, adult students don't have an alternative pathway, because young women are thought of as more likely to lie, and are seen as a threat to the precious reputations and futures of young men. So, says Bremner, survivors are placed in a "legislative black hole."

When students report a sexual assault to their universities, they can find themselves conscripted into a David-and-Goliath battle. "We're talking about nineteen-, twenty-year-old kids who have virtually no resources behind them. They're dealing with trauma, trying to stay afloat, and go to class and do all the things they need to do to graduate. While they're doing all this, they're up against these enormous institutions with just bucketloads of money, and huge legal teams that will shut down any kind of fight these kids can put up. And yet they keep going ... We're talking complaints processes that take years." Like Norvill, Sullivan, Raper and Marriot, most keep fighting for one main reason: "They just don't want it to happen to anybody else."

The problem of sexual harassment and assault on campus is, of course, not limited to the student body. Bremner is passionate about this work – she speaks forcefully but carefully when she describes the administrative systems students are up against. In conversation, she emphasises time and again not just the prevalence of individual perpetrators but also the systems protecting them. There is no record, she says, when a complaint is substantiated against a teacher, and no system for warning future employers. I mention offhand that surely, given what we learnt during the Royal Commission Into Institutional Responses to Child Sexual Abuse, educational institutions would know they need to prevent predatory teachers being moved "from parish to parish."

Her voice brightens: when *she* compared Australian universities to the Catholic Church, she was accused of hyperbole. But Bremner has receipts. "[What we saw in the Catholic Church] is exactly what we see with universities: if [abusers] do face any consequences, they are able to move, and they're able to move without any record following them. Staff can quite easily hop from uni to uni," she says. "We saw that with Peter Rathjen, the former University of Adelaide vice-chancellor. The only thing that stopped him was ICAC."

*

As we've learnt over the past four years, #MeToo stories can be long and unwieldy. By anatomising these timelines and picking through the entrails, we learn so much about not only the sexual predator being exposed, but also the culture that allowed him to be concealed and the damage that created. This chapter is primarily about federal politics, and how the government was poised to use #MeToo as a launchpad for nation-changing reforms. The following story may seem like a diversion, but the account of Peter Rathjen – his sexual misconduct at several universities, the scandal he presided over at the University of Tasmania and the way he was finally exposed – connects not only to the moment Minister Birmingham was seizing in Canberra in 2018, but also to the way #MeToo would in 2021 smash down the front doors of Parliament House.

By the time he was brought undone by the Independent Commission Against Corruption in 2020, Peter Rathjen had a decades-long history of sexual harassment, misconduct and assault. His downfall was triggered by a blog post from Michael Balter, a veteran science journalist turned #MeToo vigilante whose primary targets include predatory academics in universities around the world. In July 2019, Balter blogged that Rathjen, then Adelaide University vice-chancellor, had "a long and widespread reputation for sexual harassment going back to his earlier days as a professor," and that Balter and his "sources" would have more details soon. Despite this being an apparently open secret, it was only Balter's blog that managed to get the attention of Kevin Scarce, the chancellor at Adelaide University. Alarmed, Scarce sought advice from a solicitor, and then asked Rathjen: was there anything that he or the university should be made aware of in relation to Rathjen's past conduct? He gave Rathjen a fortnight to respond.

Three days later – in timing that could convince one of a moral universe – Rathjen was contacted by a lawyer acting for his old employer, the University of Melbourne, who told him he was being investigated for historical claims of sexual misconduct. Rathjen evidently felt no compulsion to disclose this extremely pertinent information to his chancellor. When the fortnight was up, he put Scarce at ease: there was nothing for him or the university to worry about.

It should never have been up to Rathjen to confirm or deny Balter's allegations. Since May 2018, the University of Melbourne had known about the complaint – which detailed "very serious" sexual misconduct against a female postgraduate student from 2006 to 2008, when Rathjen was dean of science. By 2019, it had substantiated it. Apparently, it never occurred to the University of Melbourne to inform the University of Adelaide that one of its senior educators had a history of sexual misconduct with a student.

Even worse, by the time Balter's blog alleged Rathjen's history of sexual misconduct, Adelaide University had already received complaints from two female employees against Rathjen. They were serious: he had, after a work function in April 2019, groped and kissed one of the women twice on the mouth. It so traumatised one of the women she ended up resigning from the university. In May 2019, Chancellor Scarce admonished Rathjen, warning him of very serious consequences if it happened again. But that was the end of it – until the complaints were referred to South Australia's ICAC.

The day after Rathjen testified to ICAC, he resigned from the university, citing "ill-health." Despite the ongoing ICAC investigation into his sexual misconduct, the university rewarded him with a payout of $326,000. By 2020, anti-corruption commissioner Brian Lander would find Rathjen guilty of serious misconduct, adding that in addition to his "egregious disrespect" for the two women he harassed, he had also lied repeatedly to both the university and to ICAC, "whenever it suited him to do so." In the wake of these findings, the blogger who originally raised the alarm echoed Sharna Bremner's "hyperbole": the report, he wrote, raised "serious questions about whether multiple institutions in Australia 'passed the harasser' despite their knowledge of Rathjen's misconduct, thus allowing him to undeservedly climb to the summits of academia."

But there was more to this story than personal misconduct. When Rathjen moved to Adelaide University from the University of Tasmania in 2017, there was another scandal exploding on his watch.

In 2014, in the middle of Rathjen's tenure as vice-chancellor at UTAS, the notorious paedophile Nicolaas Bester – on parole after being jailed for his assaults on then fifteen-year-old Grace Tame – was awarded a federally funded PhD scholarship at Tasmania's only university, UTAS. That Bester was a dangerous paedophile was beyond doubt. As Tame explains, "when he was arrested, police found twenty-eight multimedia files of child abuse material on his home computer." His assaults on Tame are now well known, but bear repeating. Bester groomed and isolated his young student for months, securing her trust enough for her to confide that, as a child, she had been locked in a closet and sexually abused. Bester, knowing that the trauma of this incident had recently caused Tame to relapse into anorexia, took her to a small, dark storeroom, locked her inside and told her to strip. This cataclysmic event led to six months of horrific sexual abuse, in which Bester – a former South African soldier who had fought in the Angolan civil war – had non-consensual sex with her twenty to thirty times on the school grounds. When Grace's anger overwhelmed her fear, she reported Bester to another teacher, who reported it to police. As Nina Funnell reported for News.com.au, when Tame's father confronted him, Bester said, "She wanted it."

When Bester received his scholarship, Tame's mother, Penny Plaschke – who had grown up working class and never had the opportunity to study – was attending university for the first time. Bester was accommodated on campus at John Fisher Campus, a co-ed student residence with shared bathrooms. When Plaschke saw her daughter's abuser on campus, she raised concerns with Rathjen "multiple times." At one point, says Bremner, Rathjen accidentally hit "reply all" on an email about the complaint, which cc'd Plaschke. "He was aware of her complaint, but basically said he had no idea what she was talking about. It was an incredibly rude, dismissive response." It was untenable for Plaschke to continue her studies with Bester on campus, so she dropped out.

Other students too had become disturbed by Bester's presence: two reports were made to police after he was seen "hanging around" the campus gym. The University of Tasmania "insisted the matter was dealt with, because Mr Bester gave up his gym membership and promised not to hang around campus cafés." Nevertheless, UTAS continued to accommodate him on campus.

In 2016, Bester was jailed again for producing child exploitation material, after he took to social media to describe his abuse of Grace in horrific detail, adding that "judging from the emails and tweets I've received, the majority of men in Australia envy me. I was 59. She was 15 going on 25 ... It was awesome." When he was released after four months, he returned to UTAS – with Rathjen still vice-chancellor – to complete his studies.

In the spring of 2017, the UTAS Women's Collective started a petition to have him banned from campus and his scholarship cancelled, arguing that allowing him to live and study on campus was putting students at risk. In May, about a fortnight before Rathjen's resignation was announced, the deputy vice-chancellor of research, Professor Brigid Heywood, defended Bester's scholarship, saying that his place at the university had been considered "with great care, with the safety of staff and students as our highest priority."

In the meantime, Bester hired a lawyer, who sent the protest organiser, student Heidi La Paglia, a laundry list of legal threats.

It was these "mounting injustices" that led Grace Tame to contact journalist Nina Funnell, who was then a director at End Rape on Campus. With Funnell, she says, she planned to tell her story, because, as she told lawyer Michael Bradley on Instagram Live, "we thought there were so many things that needed to be exposed about the culture of enabling abuse, especially in institutions." When they discovered that Tasmania's laws prohibited her from speaking publicly, Tame's case became the catalyst for Funnell's award-winning #LetHerSpeak campaign, which drew in forty survivors and survivor advocates from around Australia and changed four laws. It also led to Tame being named Australian of the Year.

Journalist and #MeToo warrior Michael Balter wrote that according to his sources, "Rathjen was instrumental in the decision to allow Bester to finish his graduate work." Meanwhile, the vice-chancellor was saying all the right things – in 2018, following a report on sexual harassment in Australian universities, the senior administrator for UTAS made a show of commitment to change: "We believe that one incident of sexual harassment is one too many." A later investigation by the University of Tasmania would unearth eleven complaints about sexual misconduct, discrimination, bullying and complaint system failures under Rathjen's leadership.

"Universities are very much run by networks of old boys," says Bremner. "And those old boys ..." She trails off, searching for the right words. "I will say, it takes a village to protect an abuser. And sometimes that village, we now know, goes all the way up to parliament. We've seen that village step in and protect over and over and over."

*

In the winter of 2018, it looked like the Turnbull government was finally ready to send an overseer to the village. Following the release of End Rape on Campus's "Red Zone" report, in which Funnell detailed shocking practices of sexual violence and hazing in Australia's residential colleges, a phone call was received from the office of Simon Birmingham, then minister of education. The "Red Zone" report had hit a nerve with the media, and Birmingham wanted to respond. The report was explicit about what was needed: a "systematic transformation" that would require, among other things, a federal taskforce with oversight over university responses to complaints of sexual assault and harassment. When Bremner and her campaign allies met with Birmingham and his staff, they were shocked by how they were received. "We came out of that first meeting going, 'What the hell just happened?' We thought we were in for a fight, and we didn't get it. Nobody expected it to go as well as it did."

Over the next few months, the taskforce developed quickly. As Bremner understood it, the taskforce would have the power to oversee university responses, paired with investigative powers to look at what universities were doing and where they were failing, and compel them to act. By August 2018, they had terms of reference, they had locked in a chair, and virtually all they were waiting on was the government to announce it. "But then Turnbull got rolled, and it all went to hell."

In late August 2018, after two dramatic leadership spills, Turnbull was replaced by his treasurer, Scott Morrison. The rise of Morrison to the prime ministership marked an abrupt end to Turnbull's narrative of gender equality and respect. Within a week, Morrison was besieged by complaints from his own female MPs – including O'Dwyer – about backroom bullying and intimidation during the leadership spill. Victorian Liberal MP Julia Banks, who had won the extremely marginal seat of Chisholm at the previous election, announced she was quitting the party, citing the events of the previous week as the "last straw." To anyone who would accuse her of "playing the gender card," she said plainly: "Women have suffered in silence for too long and in this last twelve months the world has seen many courageous women speak out." During her brief resignation speech in parliament, her male colleagues walked out. "Often when good women call out, or are subjected to, bad behaviour," she said, "the reprisals, backlash and commentary portray them as the bad ones, the liar, the troublemaker, the emotionally unstable or weak, or someone who should be silenced." The full weight of this statement became clear in 2021, when Banks revealed how Morrison – whom she would memorably describe as "menacing, controlling wallpaper" – betrayed her trust, and backgrounded against her in the days surrounding her resignation.

In Morrison's reshuffle, Birmingham was moved from Education to Trade. The new education minister was Dan Tehan, a member of Morrison's Centre-Right faction. A fortnight later, on 14 September, Senator Birmingham's former higher education adviser Darren Brown sent an email to Bremner and the team of advocates who'd been working towards the taskforce. Under the heading "Plus ça change …," he wrote: "We were so close … I have briefed the office, including Minister Tehan's [chief of staff], on where things were up to before recent developments and have passed on relevant documentation including the [terms of reference] and proposed composition of the taskforce."

It soon became clear that Tehan had no intention of picking up where Birmingham had left off. When Bremner and the other advocates travelled to Canberra to meet the new education minister, he had them see one of his advisers instead, "who couldn't have looked more bored." "We went from having meetings with the minister and working very closely with his team, to getting one meeting with Tehan's adviser … He sat slumped, so clearly uninterested. We felt like we were mosquitoes buzzing around the room, just pissing them off until we left within fifteen minutes."

Minister Tehan, it seemed, had someone more important to meet. "He met with Bettina Arndt to discuss it," says Bremner. "He personally met with Bettina Arndt. That was when I think we knew that we probably didn't want him anywhere near the issue, to be honest," she says, laughing.

Arndt – the former sex therapist, ally to anti-feminist men and long-time friend of Coalition governments – had been busy with some campus advocacy of her own. Arndt's "Fake Rape Crisis Campus Tour" – a direct riposte to the advocacy of End Rape on Campus and others – was spreading the good news that there was no rape crisis on campus.

Tehan was particularly animated by a recent run-in between Arndt and students at the University of Sydney. In September 2018, Arndt's scheduled appearance, organised by the university's Liberal Club, had been besieged by student protesters, who tried to stop attendees entering the lecture hall. Police arrived, protesters were removed and Arndt's talk went ahead. As a long-time foot soldier in the culture wars, Arndt was "thrilled," writing to supporters: "Oh Boy, we are really on a roll here. My little campus tour is causing a bit of a stir."

The meeting between Tehan and Arndt must have been productive. Instead of formalising the federal university taskforce, Tehan put it on ice and commissioned an inquiry into freedom of speech at universities – the French Review – to be led by former High Court judge Robert French (who found there was *no* freedom of speech crisis at universities).

In December 2017, as the free speech inquiry was getting underway, Arndt invited Nicolaas Bester (whom she fondly nicknamed "Nico") to have his say on her YouTube channel. Incensed at the "vigilante feminists" making his life hell at the UTAS, Arndt introducing the twice-jailed Bester as a "so-called sex offender" whose account would reveal that "these stories are often much more complex than we assume." Imploring him to tell what this "relationship" with his student had cost him, Arndt nodded sympathetically as Bester told how he'd even been recently prevented from playing the organ at his local church. Arndt concluded with a photo of a schoolgirl in a skirt and knee-high socks, noting that "over the years, I've talked to many male teachers about sexually provocative behaviour from female students. Sensible teachers, of course, run a mile from these girls, but the teachers are still really vulnerable because they can easily be subject to false accusations if they reject or offend the young woman in question." The clear inference here was that Tame was one such girl – and that although it was correct for Bester to have been imprisoned for breaking the law, the question remained for Arndt: at what point could we talk to "young girls about behaving sensibly, and not exploiting their seductive power to ruin the lives of men?"

This was the expert to whom the new education minister had given priority treatment, and whose claims he had commissioned a former High Court justice to investigate. The university taskforce was dead in the water, and the culture wars were back with a vengeance.

But neither strict defamation laws nor a change of prime minister could kill #MeToo in Australia. It just went deeper underground. Before long, events would conspire to lend the movement new momentum.

TECTONIC SHIFTS

> I don't think #MeToo can say it changed the circumstance for a cleaner who might be a recently arrived migrant, she might not speak much English, and she is being harassed by the head cleaning contractor, but she desperately needs that job. I don't think there's much about #MeToo that is reaching into her world.
>
> —Julia Gillard, January 2018

When Perlita Golding walked into The Laundry Chute to ask for a job, she had already managed to escape a violent man. As is typical, her abusive ex-husband – the father of her four children – was paying no child support, leaving Perlita to provide for their children alone in a country whose language she could barely speak. She needed to find a job that she could fit around school drop-offs and pick-ups. The Laundry Chute, next door to her English and employment services school, was conveniently located. But then another man targeted her for degradation and control. As #MeToo was taking off around the world, The Laundry Chute's owner, Ian Sippel, began to treat Golding as though she were a sex worker.

One day, after Sippel complained of a bad back, Golding (who was studying massage therapy) offered to give him a massage for $50. He offered her $500 instead for sex. A few months later, when she asked if she could borrow his lawnmower, he said yes, if she would have sex with him. In May that year, on her thirty-seventh birthday, Sippel led Golding – twenty years his junior – towards the rear of the laundromat, where he started to rub her groin through her clothes, grabbed her hand and pushed it down his shorts onto his erect penis. He held his hand over hers to masturbate himself. When Golding, afraid, told him she had to go, he said, "Can I touch yours," and shoved his hand down her pants to her vagina. Only when someone came to drop off dirty clothes was she able to get away. The assault was made worse by the fact that initially Golding had believed she could trust her boss, and had even confided in him about her ex-husband's abuse.

After the birthday assault, Sippel was emboldened. He increased Golding's shifts and would regularly ask her for sex; when she refused, he would send her away, which meant she had to beg for more work. Golding, like so many women in her position, did not have the luxury of leaving to look for other work. She *needed* this job. But working there was dangerous and traumatising. He would tell her, "You make me horny," and ask her, "When do you want to fuck me?" telling her that every time he saw her he got an erection. One afternoon, Golding was changing her clothes to go and pick up her boyfriend from the airport when Sippel approached her again. He groped the inside of her leg and told her, "One day I'm going to fuck you."

In a series of excruciating text messages in August 2018, in which Golding was requesting more hours, Sippel responded with a clear – and illegal – proposition: he would give her the hours she requested if "[you] give me your pussy." Golding left the text for hours, and then asked if he was kidding. "Maybe not," he texted back. "Maybe you give me incentive to give you the job." She didn't reply to that, and the next evening he texted, "So what you want to do?" Again, she didn't reply. Two days later he texted (as though Golding just needed some clarification), "As I can have your pussy and in turn give you job." The next morning, she replied, "Bossing [her word for boss], you already hold my pussy, I can't give that again … I holding your penis, it's enough that." The next morning, she followed up: "Please bossing, can I work?"

Sippel didn't realise he was creating an evidence trail. In August 2020, after several more incidents, Golding reported him to the police. Fearing for her safety, they advised her not to return to work. Then she took her case to Shine Lawyers.

At Shine, Golding would end up being represented by Samantha Mangwana, an employment lawyer with almost twenty years' experience in sexual harassment cases, who had only recently arrived in Australia. Of Golding's "no win, no fee" case, Mangwana says one of the fundamental advantages they had was that one of the solicitors spoke Filipino, which she says was "transformational," and at trial Golding had a translator to help her give evidence. It was a stark contrast to her experience in the criminal courts: she had no translator, no legal representation, and could barely understand what was happening. Sippel, defended by a QC, was not convicted.

"There is a different burden of proof in criminal and civil trials," Mangwana explains. "In a civil trial, you have to prove on the balance of probabilities: that 'it's more likely that it happened, than not.' The test in the criminal courts is 'beyond reasonable doubt.' If there is any reasonable element of doubt, you won't get a conviction. So when you have a victim who doesn't speak English and doesn't understand the process – that all adds to getting the necessary level of reasonable doubt."

In her civil case, Golding's testimony was almost entirely accepted. The original decision awarded her $35,000 ($30,000 to cover pain, hurt and suffering incurred by the harassment, $5000 to cover lost shifts). The commissioner set out her reasons "very carefully" – all in line with the Queensland precedent, where similarly low damages were awarded in "awful" cases. On appeal, however, the result was radically different. Justice Peter Davis, president of the Industrial Court of Queensland, assessed the original award as "manifestly inadequate" and increased the general damages to $130,000 – believed to be a "record-breaking" award in Queensland. Davis explained:

> Mr Sippel's conduct was extremely serious. Over a period of fourteen months, he tormented Miss Golding, a woman who had little choice but to work for The Laundry Chute and put up with him because of her financial position. It was that reason why she tolerated his lewd and disgusting behaviour. On every day she appeared for work, she knew the prospect was that she would be humiliated and demeaned sexually by him. That ultimately resulted in a diagnosed anxiety disorder causing her to be unable to work.

It was a "tiny footnote" in the judgment that got Mangwana's attention. There were two cases that Davis had found "of assistance" – most notably

Oracle v Richardson from 2014, which took general damages for workplace sexual harassment above $100,000 for the first time in the federal jurisdiction. "The Industrial Court of Queensland referenced two federal cases that were decided on the basis that the 'prevailing community standards' meant the ceiling on damages needed to be raised," says Mangwana. If the community standards change, then so will recognition by the courts. In Mangwana's opinion, the decision to lift Golding's damages by over $100,000 clearly illustrated the impact of #MeToo.

When her case was finalised, it was widely reported as a landmark decision. Perlita Golding bravely accepted it would go public, despite the horribly personal events in the case. She didn't want to be interviewed – she prefers that her lawyers speak for her – but "she felt that people needed to understand the violation that had happened, so that they could understand why the compensation mattered and why it was worth pursuing," says Mangwana. "It's basically saying to anyone else who finds themselves in this situation, 'You do not have to be exploited. You can fight, and you can win.'"

*

I wish we could just end on that fuzzy feeling, that the moral arc of the universe bends towards justice. But Perlita Golding is still an outlier. Pursuing sexual harassment claims is still extraordinarily risky, not least because you could, like Rebecca Richardson (of *Oracle and Richardson*), end up being ordered to pay more to your harasser's (and/or your employer's) lawyers than you get in damages – even if the sexual harassment is substantiated.

Because she refused to settle with Oracle midway through the case, Justice Robert Buchanan ordered Richardson to pay most of their legal costs, which amounted to hundreds of thousands of dollars. In that judgment, says writer and lawyer Kieran Pender, is "a really, really upsetting section where, he says, she's been vindicated, and yet, the way the law works means that she's going to face financial ruin, despite having been sexually harassed. She's sued, she won, and she was *still* going to be bankrupt. That's why she appealed – because she effectively had no choice financially." Crucially, not only did Justice Susan Kenny massively increase her damages on appeal; she also ordered Oracle to pay Richardson's costs rather than vice versa. "That story has a happy ending. But how many people either don't have a happy ending, or never get into the courtroom because of that risk?"

In a major study assessing the impact of *Richardson* in the #MeToo era, published in the *Federal Law Review*, Pender and his co-authors Madeleine Castles and Tom Hvala interviewed several legal practitioners. One was particularly blunt: "Those who think it's a nirvana post-#MeToo are in for a rude shock."

Pursuing a sexual harassment claim is not just risky – it's *hard*. Litigation is expensive and *slow*, if contested. The best case is that a complaint is resolved with a settlement for a reasonable amount but it's typically shrouded in an NDA, so the matter is never made public. And if your employer is not prepared to settle, claims can drag on for years. Even if, like Perlita Golding, you're up against a small-business owner, the fact remains: you will rarely match the resources of the individual or organisation you're up against. "It's important to improve the process of litigation," says Pender, "but it is never going to be the only answer."

Access to justice is vital. Victims should be compensated, and perpetrators (and organisations) should suffer a consequence. As Angela Lynch from Queensland Women's Legal Services puts it, "There is no prevention without accountability." But the pressure on individual victims to raise their head above the parapet and make a complaint far outweighs any pressure on employers to prevent them being harmed. Such is the risk that most victims – 83 per cent – will never report.

It's this fundamental problem that Australia's sex discrimination commissioner, Kate Jenkins, is on a mission to fix, once and for all.

*

Let's return to Gillard's statement at the opening of this chapter: can #MeToo change things for Australia's most vulnerable working women?

The answer is within the pages of Respect@Work, and in the hands of whoever forms government in 2022. The fifty-five recommendations made in Respect@Work provide the roadmap for how to protect workers from sexual harassment, but the next federal government will have to build the roads to get us there.

Jenkins handed her report to a very different government from the one that commissioned it. Turnbull and O'Dwyer were gone, and with them the commitment to improve the safety of women in Australia. When Jenkins handed Respect@Work to then attorney-general Christian Porter, its recommendations were described in the media as "paradigm-shifting" and "radical." This was not just another inquiry: through 460 submissions and more than sixty consultations involving 600 individuals, Respect@Work showed for the first time the sheer magnitude of sexual harassment in Australian workplaces – and how to fix it. As Jenkins wrote, Australia now had the opportunity to "take a leading role in the global response to sexual harassment. This is Australia's moment."

Porter, however, was not so inspired. He received it with the usual platitudes, promised to consider it carefully, and then shelved it.

Jenkins was not deterred. Instead of waiting for the government, she started shopping the report around to "workplaces that had not been decimated by Covid," and hosting webinars for anyone who showed curiosity. It would be more than a year before the government, facing a resurgent #MeToo movement, would have to respond – and only under extreme duress.

Respect@Work was blowing the roof off an open secret: an astonishing number of people are subjected to sexual harassment in Australia, and very little is done to protect them. The 2018 Australian Human Rights Commission survey found that 72 per cent of Australians had experienced sexual harassment in their lifetime and a third had been subjected to it in the workplace in just the previous five years. Certain groups were particularly targeted: Aboriginal and Torres Strait Islanders; young adults; LGBTQI and disabled workers. The term "sexual harassment" did not, for the most part, refer to the odd reckless comment or salty joke, but "a common, ongoing and habitual culture of harassment," and even sexual assault. There was something else alarming in the data: either harassers were becoming more brazen or people were better able to identify them, because the percentage of incidents witnessed by a bystander had tripled since 2012. Two-thirds of them neither intervened nor reported. Few victims complained either – only one in five (and of those, 43 per cent said they experienced a negative consequence as a result).

Respect@Work is equal parts electrifying for the future it lays out and horrifying for what it portrays. Having stared for years into the darkness of domestic abuse in Australia, I was fairly certain I'd seen the worst of us. But Respect@Work still had me reeling: the sheer volume and depravity of sexual harassment, misconduct and violence it documents is eye-watering.

One worker – a police officer – told the commission how she was travelling with colleagues when she was:

> told to lock myself in a car because I had been bought for the interstate detectives for four cartons of beer. I was given the heads up because a senior detective said I reminded him of his daughter and he wouldn't want his daughter in my situation. I woke up with some very pissed-off men licking the dew off [the] window of the police car wanting to get in. I had both sets of keys. Lucky for me.

In rural and remote workplaces, sexual harassment was shown to be so entrenched it was almost the norm. A woman working at a stock camp described "the first serious incident" she experienced:

> my manager told the contractors that the first one to have sexual intercourse with me got $1000 ... There was no mobile signal and like many stations there is only a joint landline that is shared between everyone ... I went out there wanting to learn about the basics of stockmanship and instead I was made to feel like a sex toy.

For many, there was no point complaining. As one witness put it, "There is a very strong 'Fit in or F#@* off' attitude in rural and remote Australia." This code was enforced by women as well as men: 60 per cent of the 107 victims Dr Skye Saunders interviewed for her research on sexual harassment in regional Australia said a woman contributed to their harassment.

In fact, Respect@Work documents numerous examples in which women were complicit in protecting predators, played along, or even participated in their own degradation. One worker, after reporting her harasser to a female staff member at the temp agency employing her, was told "not to make a big deal of it, because that's how they are in high finance." Another described how two young female colleagues minimised and dismissed her experience ("he's just a perv, but he's a nice guy. Don't take it so seriously") and how, when she later complained to other female staff, she was subsequently bullied out of her job, "because that's just how he is … and I took myself too seriously." There are few characters more loathed in Australian workplaces than the woman who "can't take a joke."

In a male-dominated workforce especially, said one witness, female leaders could be just as bad as the men:

> These women have been groomed and rewarded by the sexist culture. They are more interested in maintaining their status by identifying with toxic masculinity than eliminating harmful workplace attitudes and behaviour that reinforce sexual harassment.

Some women's efforts to be "one of the boys" actually did them harm. One woman working in scientific research described how she felt she had to "play along" with the "dominant culture" to have a future working alongside the predominantly male scientists. "The jokes and slurs that seemed harmless fun when we were junior researchers lodged under our skins like barbs and festered, and we were slowly poisoned by them, and by our own participation in a culture that devalued us."

Although #MeToo is primarily concerned with sexual harassment and violence against women, the inquiry found that men are also harassed.

In the majority of these cases, the perpetrator was another male or, more commonly, a group of harassers. Male victims felt it was especially hard to report when the perpetrator was female. One man told the inquiry that he felt unable to complain after a female co-worker told him, "Wife or no wife, I would fuck you in an instant," while spreading her legs and showing no panties.

As elucidated by a group of American employment lawyers in the wake of #MeToo:

> [H]arassment is not always a male-to-female phenomenon. Men harass other men who don't conform to prescribed images of who "real men" are supposed to be. Gay, lesbian, bisexual, transgender, and other people who defy traditional gender norms are subject to high rates of harassment, including physical assault. Black women and other women of color are especially vulnerable to harassment.
>
> In all these scenarios, the bottom line is that harassment is more about upholding gendered status and identity than it is about expressing sexual desire or sexuality. Harassment provides a way for some men to monopolise prized work roles and to maintain a superior masculine position and sense of self. Women, too, sometimes act to uphold their relative positions.

Respect@Work identified three characteristics that make for high-risk workplaces: male-dominated, hierarchical and/or client-facing. For women *and* men, the worst industry by far was information, media and telecommunications, with a rate of 81 *per cent*, followed by arts and recreation at 49 per cent (both well above the average rate of 31 per cent). Curiously, while women were most at risk in male-dominated industries – mining, transport, construction – men were more likely than women to report sexual harassment in workplaces such as education and training or healthcare and social assistance.

What could possibly be done to fix a problem so entrenched? Respect@Work's fifty-five recommendations aimed at one outcome: prevention.

To achieve this, the onus would need to be taken off victims of sexual harassment to complain and put squarely on employers to prevent the harassment from happening in the first place. This power imbalance – which originated in the *Sex Discrimination Act 1984* – was, Jenkins argued, central to why sexual harassment continued to flourish.

What Respect@Work recommended was that the act be amended to include a "positive duty" for employers to prevent workplace sexual harassment and bullying, with new powers to enforce compliance. Under a positive duty, employers would have no choice but to take reasonable steps to prevent workplace sexual harassment.

Does that sound radical? Unfair? Impossible?

Let's run a thought experiment. Imagine if, in Australian workplaces, turning on your computer in the morning was likely to give you an electric shock. Or you had an odds-on chance of being blinded or maimed by faulty equipment, or had to work in such poorly ventilated conditions that your co-workers would occasionally pass out on the floor.

I'm not describing a parallel reality. Aside from my hypothetical computing hazard, these *were*, until well into the twentieth century, familiar conditions for many Australian workers. Horrific physical injuries and workplace fatalities were commonplace, and until unions and collectivist workers made it impossible to ignore, employee safety wasn't a consideration for most employers and politicians. Today, the concept of work health and safety is well-established, and it's no longer controversial to say that employers are responsible for maintaining safe workplaces. This monumental shift did not come about because employers had a change of heart: it took the literal blood, sweat and tears of workers and their unions, who fought like hell for well over a century to enshrine these protections and regulations in federal legislation. While it's far from a perfect system, work health and safety laws have been incredibly successful. At the pointiest end of physical injury, results continue to improve: workplace fatalities dropped another 62 per cent from three deaths per 100,000 in 2008 to 1.1 in 2018. There's no confusion here: employers have a responsibility –

a "positive duty" – to prevent their employees from being injured at work.

The concept of workplace "injury," however, does not extend to sexual harassment. To Abbey Kendall, the wunderkind who heads the South Australian Women's Working Centre, this is "absurd." "Outside of death in the workplace, the most long-term debilitating, workplace injuries I have seen are those that are caused by sexual violence in the workplace." Kendall thinks the paradigm should be flipped: workplace sexual harassment should be considered Australia's *number one* work health and safety issue. She's represented workers across various industries, including the sparkies at the Electrical Trades Union. She's no stranger to workplace accidents – "they can be terrible injuries, and often stay with you for life" – but insists the harm is still not as debilitating as what she sees in victims of serious workplace sexual harassment. "It's the physical and mental burden of the injury you suffer from sexual harassment, as well as that additional shame and the onerous and traumatic processes in place to address an injury caused by sexual violence," she says. "That's why I think sexual harassment is our number one work health and safety issue and should be treated as such."

Remember – sexual harassment is not just unfortunate, it is *illegal*. And yet one in three Australians is subjected to it, in every conceivable workplace – from the corner store to the High Court. The harm can stay with victims for life, or at least radically reset their trajectory: many experience debilitating psychological and even physical injuries; they may be unable to work any longer in their chosen profession, they may face reputational destruction, and even financial ruin. Worse still, the process of reporting sexual harassment can end up being so punishing that victims actually get sicker from the process than from the harassment itself.

That's why prevention is key. For Kendall, the positive duty recommendation is how #MeToo would finally reach into the lives of low-paid and working-class women and change the conditions they have to suffer at work. "If that worker knew that it was unlawful, and that their employer had a positive duty to prevent sexual harassment, that would probably give them way more bargaining power."

Employment lawyer Josh Bornstein agrees. "There's a whole industry that perpetuates the mythology that if you introduce bystander training, you've made a great advance," he says. "It's horseshit. It's not about that – you need to redistribute power. [A positive duty] is worth a million bystander training programs, because it actually requires the organisation, legally, to root-and-branch consider how to minimise sexual harassment occurring. This has the capacity to get them to look at the profile of the workforce, the gender composition, wage differences. The workplaces that would most need to change are the high-risk ones: where you have men in their fifties and sixties dominating at the top, and women in their twenties and thirties down the bottom. It's potentially game-changing in that sense."

The harm from sexual harassment is clear. Respect@Work found the safety laws did impose a duty on employers to prevent sexual harassment. Clearly, this wasn't enough. Why *shouldn't* employers have a responsibility to protect their workers from it under the Sex Discrimination Act as well? That's what Respect@Work is asking the government to legislate. It is simple – and it's revolutionary.

*

When employment lawyer Samantha Mangwana migrated from the UK to Australia in January 2019, she was surprised to see that #MeToo had barely created a ripple in the legal sector here. It seemed a world away from what she'd seen go down in London. "Because it hit New York so hard, it started affecting the big US banks and law firms in London, too," she says. Mangwana remembers a lunch she had back in December 2017 with an employment lawyer for the big banks. "He said, 'Look, what's happening now is that they're actually sacking them. We're having the meetings, and they're going.'"

In the United States, #MeToo had made sexual harassment allegations so poisonous to corporate reputations and share prices that by March 2018, contracts lawyers were seeing an entirely new clause in boilerplate merger agreements. Dubbed the "Weinstein clause," it required that companies disclose any live allegations of sexual harassment, lawsuits or settlements. This was a big shift: previously, as employment lawyer Elizabeth C. Tippett wrote for *The Conversation*, harassment or discrimination were considered "small potatoes" in high-value mergers. But since Weinstein's US$200-million company had gone bankrupt in the wake of #MeToo – and lost $3.5 billion for shareholders of parent company Wynn Resorts – the risk calculation had changed.

When Mangwana arrived in Australia, she was shocked that the impact on the legal and financial professions didn't seem to have hit here, and started to question why, becoming evangelical about regulatory reforms to end the protection of known sexual harassers in law firms. But when she brought it up with her peers, most shrugged. They agreed it was a problem, and wanted it to change, "but nobody expected it would," she says. "It was like 'We know this is what happens. It's just the way it is.'"

The legal profession was about to get a very rude shock. A coming change in the weather was signalled by the International Bar Association's 2019 report, "Us Too?," which surveyed 7000 legal professionals in 135 countries – the largest survey of its kind ever conducted. The results for Australia were damning: Oceania (Australia and New Zealand) was named as the worst region for both bullying *and* sexual harassment. "That came as a massive shock," says Mangwana, "and there was a bit of backlash about it, with people saying Australians are just more prepared to report it, as opposed to us being worse than other places."

Kieran Pender led the "Us Too?" work and toured its results to twenty countries, each one at a different stage in waking up to the problem. In New Zealand, the sector had just been rocked by a massive scandal involving one of the country's most prestigious law firms, Russell McVeagh, and several senior male lawyers who had been "sexually inappropriate" with young female interns. "This was huge in New Zealand," says Pender. The New Zealanders "were saying to me, 'Tell other professions around the world to get on top of this proactively. Don't wait until there's a huge scandal.' So that was the message I was trying to share wherever I went on this campaign. You know, let's proactively make a difference. Because we *know* there's a problem." In 2019, the Australian audiences Pender spoke to were sometimes complacent. "In some quarters, there was a sense that this wasn't a major problem in the Australian profession." What they didn't know was that, inside the nation's highest court, an internal investigation was already underway into multiple allegations of sexual predation.

In June 2020, that firestorm struck. The internal investigation, ordered by Chief Justice Susan Kiefel, found that a former High Court judge, the Honourable Dyson Heydon AC QC, had sexually harassed six female associates during his time on the bench. As *The Sydney Morning Herald* would later report, Heydon's predatory behaviour had long been an "open secret." Since #MeToo, there had been a network of young women discussing Heydon, but most were afraid to come forward, even though the harassment had occurred a decade earlier. It took the rude courage of a few of Heydon's former young associates – and the High Court's first female chief justice – to bring #MeToo crashing into Australia's legal sector.

Josh Bornstein represented three of the six associates. He described the terror felt by the first woman who approached him as almost overpowering. Initially, she needed Bornstein to prove that he was not, in any way, connected to Heydon ("which I thought was funny," he says, "because Dyson Heydon and I will never be close"). This was a process he'd been through many times before, including with Tessa Sullivan, who had been similarly terrified of the reach of Robert Doyle. "It's about trying to reassure people that you're up to the task of taking on someone they believe to be all-powerful."

Heydon, who finished his term on the High Court in 2013, was known for being a "black-letter" lawyer who applied a strict interpretation of the law and detested judicial activism. As *The Sydney Morning Herald* reported, he propositioned his young associates – chosen for being among the most promising law-school graduates – repeatedly. Twenty-two-year-old Chelsea Tabart was, on the pretence of "having a drink" after a staff dinner, taken to Heydon's room, where he sat her on the couch and attempted to seduce her. When she tried to leave, Heydon suggested he go with her, saying,

"You don't know what kind of creeps are out there." He was almost fifty years her senior. Another associate, Rachael Collins, was so perturbed by Heydon's sexual advances that she did the "unthinkable" and quit as his associate to pursue studies overseas. Just before she left, after refusing several of Heydon's invitations to have a farewell dinner with him, Collins agreed to meet for a drink in his chambers. When she tried to keep her distance, Justice Heydon moved in on her, and, standing close, asked if he could kiss her. When Collins refused, Heydon demurred: "Maybe just on the cheek then?" Collins was firm. "No!" she insisted. "You're married, you're my boss. I am a practising Catholic. No."

These were allegations the Herald's investigative team, Kate McClymont and Jacqueline Maley, had been trying to report for months. But despite gathering testimonies from several women, with two willing to go on the record, it "wasn't enough to take on a High Court judge." So Bornstein, taking a chance, wrote to Chief Justice Susan Kiefel to request an internal inquiry. Given there was no precedent for such an inquiry, I wondered, was he surprised when she agreed? "Yes and no. If you're writing to the highest court in the land, about a member of the judiciary engaged in unlawful conduct during his tenure as a judge, what are their options? You're doing it post-#MeToo ... Their whole credibility and institutional support is at stake."

When the inquiry supported the women's allegations, Justice Kiefel released a statement that was brief and clear:

> The findings are of extreme concern to me, my fellow Justices, our Chief Executive and the staff of the Court. We're ashamed that this could have happened at the High Court of Australia.
>
> We have made a sincere apology to the six women whose complaints were borne out. We know it would have been difficult to come forward. Their accounts of their experiences at the time have been believed. I have appreciated the opportunity to talk with a number of the women about their experiences and to apologise to them in person.

As Rachel Doyle SC – a former High Court judge's associate herself – wrote in *Power and Consent*: in these "few terse paragraphs, an unprecedented era of soul-searching by the legal profession was ushered in."

Says Bornstein, "Dyson Heydon being exposed was the seismic event in the law. It prompted inquiries; it has made all the courts start reviewing the approach to recruitment, to relationships between staff and judges, to policies and procedures." Bornstein says he is currently representing complainants against five different judges in five different courts. "They're all falling over themselves to act decisively and properly," he says. "The courts, I think, are going through a bit of a cultural revolution."

In July 2021, Federal Circuit Court judge Joe Harman resigned following an inquiry headed by three former judges from the Supreme Court of Victoria into two complaints about sexualised and inappropriate behaviour spanning five years, back to 2015. Following the High Court's example, Chief Justice William Alstegren did not allow Harman to go quietly, instead releasing a statement to the media. The conduct was "of great concern," he said, and, echoing Kiefel, added that "the Court is ashamed that such conduct could occur." Alstegren – a conservative appointed by Christian Porter – is not someone you'd consider a natural ally of #MeToo.

Since the Heydon inquiry, *The Sydney Morning Herald* has revealed a history of predatory behaviour dating back to Heydon's time as a student at Sydney University, where "Dirty Dyson" had "an alleged propensity to grope and grab the women who crossed his path." One complainant – now a judge – was clear in her definition of what Heydon did to her. When he "slid his hands between her legs" at a professional dinner, he was committing indecent assault. Her response was clear: "Get your fucking hands off me." Speaking to the *Herald*, she said, "I have no doubt it was a crime and he knew I was not consenting."

Heydon refuses to accept the inquiry's findings and denies "any allegation of predatory behaviour or breaches of the law." In a statement, he pulled the classic "sorry not sorry," apologising if "any conduct of his has caused offence." Offence was a tellingly inaccurate term for a judge known for his exact use of language: the harm experienced by six of his associates – all brilliant young graduates – was so profound that they abandoned the legal profession entirely.

*

Not long after the Heydon inquiry became public, #MeToo rocketed through the financial services sector. AMP shareholders revolted when it was revealed that the newly promoted head of AMP Capital, Boe Bahari, had been penalised $500,000 in 2017 for sexually harassing Julia Szlakowski, then an institutional director working for him. When AMP used public relations to minimise the harassment – which had left Szlakowski so disturbed she would wake up screaming in bed, paralysed with anxiety, and stopped eating to such a degree that she lost nine kilos – Szlakowski outed herself. As her lawyer, Josh Bornstein, observed, the fact that she had not signed a non-disclosure agreement allowed her to "defend [her] reputation by setting the record straight." Boe Pahari was demoted, while AMP chairman David Murray and chief executive Francesco De Ferrari both resigned.

Jenkins says it was the Heydon revelations first and foremost – buttressed by ICAC's investigation into senior educator Peter Rathjen and the shareholder revolt against AMP's Pahari – that pushed Respect@Work onto the government's agenda. "This is why it is important to have these public high-profile cases become public – for the change they can achieve." However, just as crucial as Heydon's high-profile scalp was the way the chief justice made the entire profession – not just him –accountable. "Instead of Susan Kiefel saying, 'There's one bad judge,' she said: 'We're ashamed this happened here.' It was a show of leadership for the profession. So all the courts, the tribunals – the entire legal sector – started realising, 'Oh, we're a part of this,' which was massive compared to how they'd always dealt with sexual harassment in the past. Now the pressure is on to be transparent, and to take action."

Following this peak of interest, introspection and inquiries, are there signs the Heydon inquiry has sparked enduring structural change? Kieran

Pender says, "The courts have really grappled with this – but they're [at] the apex of the profession. I think the impact on the rest of the legal sector has been more varied." As he sees it, the impact cannot be measured by what happens this year or next, but by whether this is still a live issue in years to come. "We don't change social behaviour overnight, we do it via a long and enduring campaign. And so I worry that as soon as it's no longer the flavour of the month, we'll backslide, and we won't get as far as we need to."

*

In the final months of 2020, an unusually thin episode of *Four Corners* went to air. Titled "Inside the Canberra Bubble," it portrayed a federal parliament populated by conservative ministers who moralised by day, philandered by night. It was certainly disturbing in what it revealed about abuses of sex and power inside Parliament House, but curiously light on detail. Aside from the powerful testimony of Rachelle Miller, who described how she had been humiliated and belittled in the office by her boss, Alan Tudge, while they were having a consensual affair, there was little but vague insinuations of a culture rife with sexism, sleaziness, bullying and inappropriate behaviour.

Little else, aside from a curious focus on the then attorney-general, Christian Porter. ABC journalist Louise Milligan had sought out friends and associates of Porter back when he was at university, to portray a man with a known history of virulent sexism. But what did Milligan have to connect the young Porter to the adult attorney-general? Not much, aside from the fact he'd been sighted by half of Canberra openly cavorting with a young woman who was not his wife, and was subsequently warned by his prime minister, Malcolm Turnbull, that such careless behaviour could leave him open to use of *kompromat* by foreign agents. That was a salacious tidbit, but it didn't seem to warrant such a deep dive into Porter's history. It was catnip to the ABC's critics, who decried the episode as a hatchet job, and gave ammunition to those who saw it as a gratuitous incursion into the traditionally private lives of politicians. It was, in the #MeToo context, reminiscent of the Aziz Ansari story – it clearly struck a nerve, and sparked conversations about the culture of parliamentary offices, but much of the debate that followed centred on whether it should ever have been told at all.

The Friday after the episode went to air, Milligan hinted at what may have been left on the cutting-room floor. Speaking at the launch of her book *Witness*, she described the extreme level of government interference over the story, comparing it to the "siege mentality" of the Catholic Church. "They went over our heads," she said. "And they didn't just go to the executive producer of the program or the director of news. They went to the managing director and the board and tried to editorially interfere in the national broadcaster. This is the sort of institutional power that you come up against when you try to expose this sort of behaviour."

As Australians would soon learn, the main story Milligan had wanted to tell was missing, spiked by ABC lawyers at the eleventh hour. It wasn't just the story that was missing from the episode, however, but the woman who would have told it.

In 2019, Kate Thornton – a historian working on her PhD – started to reach out to old friends. She was looking for supportive people who had known her back in university – back when she had been lauded for her brilliance as a debating champion and had the world at her feet. She knew she would need support, because she was preparing to go public with an allegation against one of the nation's most senior lawmakers.

One of Kate's old friends was Jo Dyer, a theatre and film producer, and director of Adelaide Writers' Week. Dyer had known Kate since Year 10, when they met trying out for the South Australian debating team. Jo remembers the young Kate as a warm, charismatic girl with "sharp intelligence, rigorous intellect … [and] compelling eloquence." In the world of debating – populated by many precocious talents – Kate "shone … as one of the brightest." In 1988, she was selected as captain of the national schools debating team, joining an elite tradition that had given rise to some of Australia's leading journalists, academics, television stars and politicians. One had, by 2019, become the federal attorney-general. It was this man Kate was planning to go public about.

"I really believe that she was done with living with it," Dyer tells me. "She had tried to bury it, to move beyond it, but ultimately she just couldn't." When Dyer met up with Kate all those years later, she was a "very different person." As Dyer would later tell the ABC, "the thing that you would notice about K[ate] was that she was caught on a jag, in a very specific era, around a very specific incident ... She was consumed with a trauma which she told me, deeply and consistently, was as a result of an assault that had occurred early in 1988. Her life [had become] really devoted to exploring how she could get some kind of justice, accountability and peace from that ... There was still a burning passion there, but it was to try to rectify a wrong."

In years gone by, Kate's allegation may have been written off as conspiratorial. But #MeToo had radically altered the community's response to such stories about powerful men. Dyer believes that after #MeToo, Kate saw "an opportunity for her to speak and be heard and believed that she didn't think had existed before."

Kate also knew she was in danger. She had been diagnosed bipolar and had attempted suicide several times. "She talked about that quite openly," says Dyer. "She understood she was at risk of dying by suicide. She thought this could help."

The allegation of assault Kate described to her friends has been strenuously denied by Christian Porter. The details are contained in a 31-page dossier, which Kate's friends say she had prepared to hand over to police. It was published by the Federal Court in June 2021. In it, Kate describes, in sometimes excruciating detail, what she says Porter did to her.

The following account is graphic, confronting and disturbing. We present it here because, despite the dossier's status as an allegation, the absence of any formal investigation that could establish a legal rejection or acceptance of the allegations means the possibility of it being true abides in the public imagination equally with the possibility of it being a false and unreliable account. We make no comment here as to the reliability or veracity of the allegations detailed.

In the early hours of 10 January 1988, Kate alleged, Porter raped her three times. They had both been selected, with two others, for the Australian schools debating team, and were in Sydney for the World Universities Championships. Before they were to attend a formal dinner, Porter brought his shirt over to Kate's room for her to iron. As he sat watching her, he told her she was "so smart and so pretty" but could do all the "good housewife things." Porter said that this was exactly the kind of wife he would need to help his political career. Kate was flattered – by all accounts, Porter was charismatic, charming and good-looking – and believed Porter was suggesting that she personally would be an ideal wife for him. They went to dinner, then out dancing, and then Porter walked Kate back to her room at the Women's College at Sydney University. Kate suspected, but couldn't prove, that Porter had slipped some "date-rape style drug" into her drink, because her memories of what happened next had a "surreal quality."

When they got to her room, she wrote, Porter asked, "How about a pearl necklace?" Kate, who was still a virgin, had never heard of the term, but presumed it was something sexual. She said that when Porter failed to orgasm, he told her she couldn't just leave him "with blue balls." He then forced Kate to perform oral sex on him. Kate said no repeatedly, saying, "Please don't make me" and "No, I don't want to." She wrote that Porter then kicked her in the knee, pushed her to the ground and stood in front of her, putting his penis in her mouth. "He had his hands around my throat, I thought that he would choke me to death." As Porter pulled her by the hair, she heard the sound of ambulance sirens outside. "Dissociating badly, in order to cope," she lost track of time, and when he ejaculated into her mouth, she vomited. Porter then took her to the shared bathrooms, ran her a bath, and not only washed Kate, but shampooed her hair twice, and shaved her legs and armpits. In the steamed-up mirror, with Kate crying behind him, she said he wrote "Christian Porter was 'ere Jan 88."

Still drunk and exhausted, Kate found it hard to stand up, and Porter took her back to her room, and dressed her in her pyjamas. "As I was falling asleep in CP's arms, he was whispering to me, as if I were a toddler who had woken up in the middle of a nightmare 'shoosh, shoosh, shoosh, shoosh, Katie, shoosh. Don't cry, go back to sleep, it's all just a bad dream. I've got you. I'll stay with you until you fall asleep.'" When she woke up, she wrote, she was naked, lying face down, and Porter was anally raping her. All she can remember him saying to her was "I don't want to get you pregnant." She passed out. Shortly afterwards, she claimed, Porter anally raped her again. To her later shame, she experienced an "intense multiple orgasm," which is why she felt unable to report the rape to anyone the next day. Later that morning, she woke up alone, and found she was bleeding rectally.

As a sixteen-year-old trying to cope, she reassured herself that maybe things had gone "a bit too far" the night before, but that was okay, because they were going to get married one day. She spent the next day with Porter, visiting a friend. The next time she saw him, in 1994, she was revolted by several "inappropriate remarks" he made towards her, but also relieved. "I felt shaken, but relieved, as if I had broken a spell that had been cast some seven years earlier."

In 2019, supported by several friends from her debating days, Kate decided to report the alleged assault to police. She knew the likelihood of securing a criminal conviction was low. She also knew there would be a cost if it became public, and had conversations with Dyer about the blowback that would inevitably come from News Corp. But she was determined to go through with it, regardless. It was important to her that her statement be placed on the record and be kept in the police archives. "My original training was as an historian," she wrote. "This is my story, plain and simple. It's not pretty, but it's mine."

After several conversations with police in South Australia and New South Wales, Kate decided to record her statement with police in Adelaide, where she would have emotional support. In March 2020, as Covid-19 hit, NSW Police (in whose jurisdiction the alleged assault had taken place) had received approval to travel to Adelaide to take Kate's statement. But the final approval, required from Deputy Commissioner David Hudson, was denied – ostensibly due to Covid-19 restrictions, and "insufficient detail ... to justify why this travel cannot be deferred." To this day, Dyer is mystified by the decision. "We were told there was an edict that only essential interstate travel was allowed," she says, "and that's actually not true. It was only essential international travel that wasn't allowed; interstate travel was absolutely still allowed. You just needed to have a deputy commissioner sign off on it. And that was him. He made a decision not to."

In the months following, Kate spiralled. "She had been screwing her courage to the sticking post. This had been a difficult path to tread, which is why she was reconnecting with so many different people from her past, but also bolstering herself with institutional support, like Marque Lawyers. There had been this steady progress, a forward momentum, and then it all just came grinding to a halt." That was the moment, according to Kate's partner, that she started to deteriorate mentally. The cancellation of the police visit was compounded by another significant event in April, when Cardinal George Pell successfully appealed his conviction for historical sex crimes in the High Court. "The fact that this was a case of historical rape where the story had initially been enough, and then it was overturned ... Those were the two key things that derailed her."

In May, Kate voluntarily admitted herself into a psychiatric hospital in Melbourne, where she stayed for just under a month. When she came back to Adelaide, Covid-19 travel conditions meant she had to isolate alone at home. A few days later, she called NSW Police to tell them she would not be pursuing her complaint. She did not recant her story, nor withdraw her allegations. The next day, after cutting her hair into the style she had been wearing when she was photographed with Porter in 1988, Kate went out into her backyard and hanged herself.

A day or two later, Kate's phone rang. It was her lawyer, Michael Bradley, calling to see if she would be interested in talking to Louise Milligan from the ABC. Milligan had for a while been hearing about a mystery woman, talked about in Liberal circles, but had only just twigged that they shared a mutual friend, Nick Ryan. Through Ryan, Milligan had got on to Bradley. In the end, Milligan heard about Kate's death before Bradley did and, in a terrible turn of events, ended up being the one to inform him that his client was dead.

Dyer says the timing was tragic. "I firmly, 1000 per cent, believe that if Louise had managed to track down Kate even just forty-eight hours before she did, then Kate would still be alive. It would have absolutely transformed her thinking about everything. She missed her by maybe thirty-six hours at the most."

*

Seven months later, on a summer's night in Canberra, Grace Tame was named the Australian of the Year for catalysing Nina Funnell's #LetHerSpeak campaign. Taking the stage next to the prime minister, Tame was electric. "I remember him [Bester] saying, don't tell anybody. I remember him saying, don't make a sound. Well, hear me now, using my voice amongst a growing chorus of voices that will not be silenced. Let's make some noise, Australia!"

As Tame finished her speech, standing in front of the country's media, Morrison leaned over and said in her ear, "Well, gee, I bet it felt good to get that out."

When young Canberra staffer Brittany Higgins saw Morrison onstage with Tame that night, she felt sick. "He's standing next to a woman who has campaigned for 'Let Her Speak' and yet in my mind his government was complicit in silencing me. It was a betrayal. It was a lie." She quit her job as a media adviser and prepared to go public with her own allegations.

By March 2021, these three women – Kate Thornton, Grace Tame and Brittany Higgins – would trigger a resurgent #MeToo movement in Australia, and a citizen-led insurgency against the Morrison government.

INSURGENCY

Katharine Murphy had never seen anything like it. In her twenty-five years in the Canberra press gallery, she could recall no precedent for the scenes she witnessed at Parliament House in the first few months of 2021. "It's hard to convey in words. It was like the lid blew off the place." Frustrations building for decades had found a human face in one complainant, and triggered "the most incredible reaction through the building," says Murphy, political editor at *Guardian Australia*. "I'd go downstairs to get a coffee, and staff who I had never even spoken to would approach in tears, either with stories or gratitude for the fact that reporters were sticking with the story. There was an incredible collective sense of grief, and responsibility."

That one complainant – at least, at the beginning – was former Coalition staffer Brittany Higgins. When Higgins went public, the horror of her allegation was almost too much to bear. What she had alleged – a rape in a federal minister's office – was harrowing. But the moral cowardice of the government she worked for – the officials we elected – was truly grotesque. Instead of being treated as a valued staffer – as a human being – Higgins was dealt with as a political problem. The man in question was fired within days, sacked for a "security breach," the minister, Linda Reynolds, would claim, although both staffers had signed in at the front desk, as was standard practice. A week after the alleged rape, Reynolds invited Higgins to her office to discuss it – the same office Higgins said she had been raped in. In the following days, home affairs minister Peter Dutton was briefed, as were staff in the prime minister's office. Higgins filed an informal report to the AFP, who also met with Minister Reynolds to discuss it. After the federal election in May that year, Higgins worked with the employment minister, Michaelia Cash, who said she didn't find out about the alleged rape until February 2021, despite a journalist inquiring about it, several meetings on how to handle it, and sympathetic voicemails left with Higgins in 2019 that indicate the contrary. And at the end of it all, when Samantha Maiden broke the story on News.com.au on

15 February, there was a shocked prime minister, Scott Morrison, who said nobody had ever told him. Nobody – not his defence industry minister, his home affairs minister, his employment minister, his own staff – had felt that an alleged rape in a ministerial office warranted his attention. To former senior Coalition figures, this was clearly preposterous – or evidence of a severely abnormal leadership culture. "In my experience, a serious indictable offence would be brought to the attention of the prime minister immediately," said former deputy leader Julie Bishop, in typically diplomatic form. Former prime minister Malcolm Turnbull was more blunt: "I find it incredible, that's to say very, very, very hard to believe, that the prime minister's office would not have been aware of that incident as soon as it occurred."

Nonetheless, that was the story Morrison expected the public to accept. He did concede failings, once his wife, Jenny, had urged him to look at the situation "as a father first." He announced reviews – the Foster review, the Hammond review – and tasked the head of his department, Phil Gaetjens, with investigating who knew what, when. All above board, everything neat and tidy.

Until three days later, when Network Ten political editor Peter van Onselen reported that Morrison's office had been backgrounding journalists against Higgins' partner, David Sharaz – a former public servant who, they were saying, had a gripe with the government. Morrison announced another review – the Kunkel review – to investigate. It was not possible, apparently, for the leader of the nation to pull his own staff aside and ask them about it.

And then the second bomb exploded, less than a fortnight after the first. ABC journalist Louise Milligan had finally found a way to tell the missing story from "Inside the Canberra Bubble." On 26 February she revealed that a letter detailing an historical rape allegation against an unnamed federal cabinet minister had been sent to the prime minister, and referred to the Australian Federal Police. Overnight, sixteen male cabinet ministers became rape suspects. Morrison seemed untroubled. He'd discussed it with the minister accused, who had rejected the allegations. He'd consulted with various officials: there were "no matters that require my immediate attention." Turning incuriosity into performance art, Morrison had apparently been sent Kate's unsigned statement, but had not read it. After all, the victim was deceased – what more was there to say?

But Kate had her representatives, and they got to work. On 7.30, Jo Dyer explained why she believed her. "The detail that she recounted, the lucidity with which she recounted it, and the clear impact that it had had on her – all of these things persuaded me immediately that she was telling the truth." Dyer was unequivocal: there would need to be an independent inquiry. Referring to Kate's network of friends, many of whom had become powerful figures in banking and conservative politics, Dyer said, "We are happy to stand here and argue that case for her."

On 3 March, the unnamed cabinet minister outed himself. Red-eyed and shaking, Attorney-General Christian Porter emphatically denied the allegations, claimed that no journalists had ever put the details to him (despite several insisting they had) and said that he had been put on public trial. He refused to step down, announcing instead that he would be taking two weeks off for his mental health. To the journalists before him, and the voters beyond, he pleaded: "Just imagine for a second that it isn't true."

To the lawyer who represented Kate in the months before she died, this was the moment everything started to go wrong for Porter. "You're doing this to an Australian audience – most people would have been like, *mate, suck it up. If you say it didn't happen, fine. Face it!* There was an obvious course of action: stand down, have an inquiry. If anyone has the platform to argue their corner and restore their reputation, it's the attorney-general," says Michael Bradley, managing partner at Marque Lawyers. "I think he played it extremely badly."

The "cultural revolution" in the courts in 2020 apparently had no influence on the country's chief lawmaker, nor any sway over the prime minister. The obvious model for an inquiry had been established by the chief justice of the High Court, Susan Kiefel, with the Heydon investigation. What's more, Porter had not only endorsed that process, but even promised to expand it. Nonetheless, the hyperbole machine went into overdrive: such an inquiry would be a rejection of law and order, Morrison chided, and the attorney-general would not be stood down. "Terrible things ... can happen in a country where the rule of law is not upheld." Dyer, appearing again on 7.30, was impish: the chief justice of the High Court had not thought such an inquiry would "catapult us into a lawless state."

Into this fevered scene another incendiary device was launched. A former private school student, Chanel Contos, put a call out on Instagram in February to see if any of her followers had been sexually assaulted by someone at an all-boys school. Contos herself had been – in fact, as she was realising, sexual assault among her friendship group was virtually the norm. By March, she had received more than 5000 testimonies – some from students as young as thirteen – describing sexual assault, coercive control, rape and abuse. Although stories also poured in from public schools, Contos had elite single-sex schools in her sights: the production line of power that has educated the vast majority of Australia's most powerful CEOs, and eight of the last eleven prime ministers. The testimonies painted a damning picture of male entitlement: a predatory culture, steeped in hardcore porn, within which sexual assault had become not the exception but the rule at student parties on weekends. Private-school girls wrote of being raped while they were unconscious, forced to perform oral sex, pressured to have threesomes, and having images taken without their consent and shared online. Sometimes, these were boys they'd just met; other times, close friends. "It happened to so many of us," Contos told *The Sydney Morning Herald*. "We talk about a guy who forced us to give them head like [we talk about] what we had for breakfast yesterday." Of the public shock at the volume of these testimonies, she said: "Australia has woken up to the fact we live in rape culture."

*

The momentum seemed to be with #MeToo. But this wasn't like 2017, when the blowtorch was aimed at a few Australian celebrities. In 2021, #MeToo was presenting an existential threat to the federal government, and specifically to one of its most promising senior ministers: a man touted as a future prime minister. Porter's task now was to undo the central moral accomplishment of #MeToo, and what it had given to Kate: the benefit of the doubt.

The attacks began on 5 March, three days after Porter named himself, and started in a place many least expected: the independent news website Crikey. The piece, by David Hardaker, was riddled with errors and based on a false premise: that Kate had only "remembered" Porter raping her after she sought therapy in 2019 (although she had actually disclosed to a therapist in 2013, and had kept contemporaneous notes in her diaries). The article was brimming with conjecture, suggesting that it was *after* Kate read *The Body Keeps the Score* – a bestselling book on trauma – that images of her rape had been unleashed in her psyche, leading her to take her life nine months later. The therapy she had undergone, known as EMDR, was dismissed as "pseudoscience," despite being so routine in trauma therapy that it's covered by Medicare. Having created this haphazard trail, Hardaker asked the woefully misinformed question: "Is it possible that the discredited and dangerous practice of recovered memory has now ensnared an attorney-general?"

The following week, in *The Australian* on 12 March, came an "exclusive" from Janet Albrechtsen and Peter van Onselen, the latter a long-time friend of Porter, publishing several of Kate's diary entries (previously sent to South Australian police and various politicians). The entries were visceral and disturbing: "Please Do Not Take Me" she writes, using one word per page. It was the most detailed account yet of Kate's allegations, and the authors were guiding their readers towards a particular conclusion: that these diary entries were the product of a sick mind and must therefore cast doubt on her allegations.

Three days later, Porter announced, while still on mental-health leave, that he would be suing the ABC for defamation. In his statement of claim, there was a telling paragraph: he was accusing the ABC and Milligan of selecting portions of Kate's dossier that made the "allegations appear as credible as possible when there were other significant portions of the dossier which demonstrated that the allegations were not credible." As *The Age* journalist Benjamin Millar noted on Twitter, remarkably, in the days preceding this claim, there had been a "flurry" of articles featuring these "other portions" of Kate's dossier. Tweeted Millar: "PVO and JA take a hatchet to the alleged victim on Saturday, Andrew Bolt does the same in today's *Herald Sun* and now Sharri [Markson] has the exclusive drop on the defamation. This is all hands on deck stuff."

The strategy seemed clear. "This takes pressure off the govt to call its own inquiry and helps frame CP as the victim," Millar tweeted. "The focus becomes more about reputational damage and the ABC acting with 'malice.' Narrative of the unreliable (mentally unstable) accuser will only get louder from here."

This tactic is so textbook it has its own acronym: DARVO, which stands for Deny, Attack and Reverse Victim and Offender. It works like this: the alleged perpetrator – and their supporters – denies the allegation, attacks the victim's credibility and then reverses the roles of victim and offender to present the alleged perpetrator as the real victim. The attack is intended to chill and terrify the victim and their supporters, and it often includes legal threats. It's usually very effective: research has shown that not only does a DARVO response make observers less likely to believe the victim, it also makes victims more likely to feel themselves at fault.

This time, however, it backfired spectacularly. The intention to discredit Kate was clear, and the response to it was ferocious. Ironically, many who read the *Australian* piece regarded the diary entries as evidence that supported Kate's allegations. In a *Crikey* article, Dr Leslie Cannold wrote: "There is something exquisitely screwed up about a society that abuses women in ways that cause trauma, and then uses the mental illness that trauma can provoke as evidence that they were never really abused in the first place."

Bradley says this attempt to undermine Kate was Porter's next big mistake. "They went directly to the playbook of victim-blaming and using whatever was available to paint her as an unreliable witness, and did it in a really grubby way," he says. "Since all this blew up, every step Porter has taken has been about controlling the story and getting his narrative out there – but spectacularly unsuccessfully. The more he's dug down, the more harm he's done himself."

Porter's defamation announcement came the same day as rage was peaking around the nation. That Monday, 15 March, an estimated 110,000 people marched, in forty cities and towns, for "justice," in a spontaneous demonstration triggered by Higgins, Porter and Contos. It's hard to convey how electrifying this day felt: the feeling of fury and willpower being unleashed, of a collective rage and rebellion and raw emotion pouring into the streets. In Sydney, as I walked with my mother-in-law, Lorraine, along Macquarie Street, I had rarely seen her look so alive. On street corners, people stopped just to talk; women disclosed traumas they had kept quiet their whole damn lives to perfect strangers – strangers they trusted, because the collective trauma of February and March had created among us a kind of familial bond.

On the lawns in front of Parliament House, at the Canberra March 4 Justice rally, Brittany Higgins made a surprise appearance. To a cheering crowd, she said that since going public, she had watched as her former colleagues – people to whom she had dedicated her professional life – downplayed her lived experience. "I have read the news updates every day at 5 a.m. because I was waking up to new information about my own sexual assault through the media," she said. "Details that were never disclosed to me by my employers, information that would have helped me with questions that have haunted me for years. I watched as people hid behind throwaway phrases like 'due process' and 'presumption of innocence.'"

She ended her speech with a message that would be echoed at rallies across the country: "I encourage each and every one of you to set boundaries for yourself and be ruthless in your defence of them. Speak up, share your truth and know that you have a generation of women ready, willing and able to support you. Take ownership of your story and free yourself from the stigma of shame."

In Question Time, the prime minister – who had refused to go out to meet the march, and whose offer to meet privately had been turned down by the organisers – said it was "good and right" that so many could meet peacefully to express their "very genuine and real frustrations." Not far from here, he added, "such marches, even now, are being met with bullets but not here in this country, Mr Speaker."

A week later, on 22 March, after a political staffer was found to have filmed himself masturbating on the desk of a female MP, Morrison clearly realised his stonewall approach was not working. As Laura Tingle acidly put it on 7.30, "Suddenly, the enormity of the political trouble the prime minister is in, the sense of crisis and paralysis, the unravelling of too-clever political management and, of course, a masturbatory offence against a piece of furniture, seemed to have finally, if briefly, prompted Scott Morrison today to engage all those skills learned in his taxpayer-funded empathy training." His attempt to hit the reset button – a passionate mea culpa address to the nation – would do more, as laid out in my introduction, to reveal him than it would to absolve him. That night, long-time Liberal MP Russell Broadbent looked mortified as he spoke to 7.30 in his parliamentary office. "I mean, Australia must be disgusted with us at the moment," he said. "It's just so embarrassing. I'm embarrassed ... the young women working in my office in Warragul, their parents must be saying to them, 'What have you got yourselves into here?'"

By March, it was clear that there was something very different in the way this story was being covered. It was not just that it was being doggedly pursued by a number of senior female press gallery journalists – most visibly Tingle, Niki Savva, Samantha Maiden and Katharine Murphy – but that these female journalists were unswayed by the usual tactics. This was not the same press gallery that had covered Gillard. "I certainly learnt lessons after the Gillard era," Murphy tells me. She's thought on this a lot over the years and is determined "not to repeat the mistakes of that period." Though the sexism in Gillard's treatment had been clear at the time, Murphy says she (and, I would add, virtually the entire gallery) "had not leaned into that sufficiently." Partly it was because, back then, writing about politics through a gendered lens was not the done thing, particularly for senior female journalists, but also, as Murphy says candidly, it was because she just didn't want to believe it was happening.

"For a woman of my generation, you think, okay, feminism has got us so far – not to parity, obviously – but *so* far. We're at the table, we're in leadership positions, and I am the beneficiary of this work. I *believed* that fundamentally, there had been progress. And it wasn't until I lived through that period that I worked out things hadn't changed. We hadn't, in fact, made it better for our own daughters. It's an experience that resets you, right?"

*

By the end of March – after another Coalition MP, Andrew Laming, had been accused of tormenting female constituents online – Christian Porter had been quietly shuffled out of the office of attorney-general and into the portfolio of industry, science and technology. A newly branded suite of portfolios was named under a "Cabinet Taskforce" for women's equality, safety, economic security, health and wellbeing. It was Reset 2.0, as Morrison stepped out with his newly minted attorney-general, Michaelia Cash, to – after thirteen months – respond to Respect@Work. The prime minister described the inquiry as a "game changer" – but soon revealed that he was not. The government agreed, wholly or in part, to the bulk of the recommendations, except for the most important one: the positive duty. What's more, despite pledging $3.2 billion to women in the federal budget, and despite "presiding over a government during which rates of sexual harassment have *increased*," the Morrison government failed to give funding certainty to the country's three remaining Working Women's

Centres. Funding a centre in every state and territory was a recommendation in Respect@Work. Now there was no guarantee the centres would survive the year.

Events were beginning to slow, and Covid-19 was back on the horizon, but #MeToo was not finished with 2021 yet. In April, at a time when public conversation about consent had never been so sophisticated, the government dropped a new consent education package. Called "The Good Society," it contained 350 resources and cost $3.7 million (part of the Respect Matters funding package announced by Turnbull in 2015). For a suite of resources about sex, it made remarkably little mention of actual sex; instead, there were tortured metaphors about milkshakes, tacos and shark-infested waters. It was even disavowed by Nationals senator Matt Canavan: "I'm no expert in this field," he told the ABC, "but I think these sort of clumsy metaphors probably do make more confusion for young children than help." Despite the government claiming the program had been developed in conjunction with Our Watch and Foundation for Young Australians, both organisations denied being consulted on the final product. When Contos showed the videos to friends in London, they thought it was satire.

But it wasn't a joke. Nina Funnell said it was "actually extremely distressing to think about how much money went into that, and what could have been achieved with something that was actually evidence-based. At the end of the day, people are actually being raped. To think that there are these pots of money just being pissed up against the wall … it's not just heartbreaking. It's a travesty."

By the end of May, the "defamation trial of the century" was discontinued by Porter, and both sides agreed to a decidedly less flashy compromise: an editor's note on Milligan's original online story to say that it did not contend that the allegation could be substantiated to a legal standard and regretted that "some readers misinterpreted the article as an accusation of guilt against Mr Porter." This was the only concession – no damages were paid, the reporting remains online, and the ABC bore only the costs of the mediation. It was, to put it mildly, anti-climactic.

Just when it seemed that #MeToo's momentum was easing, former Coalition MP Julia Banks dropped her long-awaited memoir, three years after her spectacular resignation from the Liberal party. In an extraordinary interview on 7.30, Banks revealed that when she had gone to Morrison with her intention to resign from the party in 2018, he had pleaded with her to give him twenty-four hours. She agreed, believing the request was made in good faith. "That was my first mistake," she said. Very soon, Banks saw that the story of her resignation was leaking, and after twenty-one hours released her own statement.

"And then Morrison rang me and he said, 'You agreed on twenty-four hours.' He was a bit cross about that, and I said the story was leaking. And then he said, 'Well, I'll tell you what we'll do, I'll come to your electorate and we'll do a press conference together,' and I said, 'No, no, Scott, I'm taking a few days' leave.' He said, 'Well, do me a favour, do not speak to the media. Don't do any interviews.' And I agreed to that. And that was my second mistake." Banks didn't know then that the prime minister's office was already backgrounding the press on her mental health – "That I had had a complete sort of emotional breakdown, I had not coped with the coup."

At a press conference soon after, when Morrison was asked about Banks not recontesting, Banks remembered "watching the television and thinking, 'What's he saying?'" Morrison was positioning her. "What am I doing right now? I'm supporting Julia, and I'm reaching out to Julia, and giving her every comfort and support for what has been a pretty torrid ordeal for her."

Banks was irate: "He's very good at controlling the narrative," she explained. When Laura Tingle asked why she ultimately decided to leave parliament, Banks landed the killer blow. "I left because … I realised Morrison, the most powerful man in the country … wanted me silenced. He wanted me to be quiet."

*

There was one more woman who would not be quiet. Throughout 2021, Grace Tame had been touring the country, educating audiences on grooming and child sexual abuse, and campaigning for the legislative changes she had set out to achieve, including harmonising the definitions of consent, which vary from state to state.

Standing next to the prime minister in January, when she was named Australian of the Year, had been surreal. "There were so many things that were going on for me in that moment. Disbelief that it was even happening – to be named Tasmanian of the Year is out of this world, but then to be named Australian of the Year? That was just ridiculous, in the best way possible. Because like, literally eleven years ago, I was lying on my back wishing I was dead. And then I was standing up and being recognised and celebrated for *that very story* – you know, that is just a crazy 180." She looks back on the woman who stood on that stage and sees that even as she was trying to explain to people that "we've been groomed as a society, there was still so much naivety."

Her evolution, from someone with little understanding of politics to a key player within it, has happened at breakneck speed. For the first few months, Tame would drop the odd remark calling out members of the government, but remained, at her core, optimistic and open. By August 2021, battle-hardened, Tame had become a full-blown insurgent.

On 2 August, when Porter was returned to the role of acting leader of the House of Representatives, Tame was incensed: "It's hard to process how an accused rapist – albeit one who will never face prosecution – could be offered one of the highest positions of power in the country by none other than our nation's leader himself," she wrote in *The Sydney Morning Herald*. "Last week I had what I thought was a productive meeting with the federal government, and now this has happened. I'm not party-political, but I call out injustice where I see it, and in this instance, it is damn near blinding."

Tame, with her devastating precision and no-fucks attitude, is one of a generation of young women who are not waiting for a pat on the head, who will not fade quietly into the grey area. "I just call shit how I see it," Tame says. "And it just so happens that this current government will not properly address the issue of sexual assault within its own ranks."

Associate Professor Mike Salter, one of the country's leading experts on child sexual abuse, is amazed by the example Tame has set this year – and by what she's achieved, expanding the discussion of child sexual abuse beyond specific incidents, to show the entire system of grooming and control. "All of a sudden, sexual violence is not an incident," he says, "sexual violence is this controlling process of which sexual activity is *one* part."

This is the work of not just #MeToo, but "me too." The work that Tarana Burke envisioned back in 2007 – of education, of solidarity, of *healing*. Because, ultimately, politics will come and go. But true leadership – the kind that unites communities, that heals the hurt – that is what we are all yearning for. It is what #MeToo should stand for. It is what Tame has been fighting for this year, at enormous personal cost. When I ask her how she is holding up, she tells me straight. "I was in the ER a couple of months ago," she says. "I'm living constantly on the precipice of a shame state from the retraumatisation."

But Tame does not dwell on what it costs her to do this work. She has a wicked sense of humour and becomes particularly animated when our conversation turns to Christian Porter. In a 1600-word statement when he resigned as cabinet minister in September, he not only sought to undermine Kate, but blamed the ABC and the "Twitter mob" for his downfall. He will, however, contest the next election. "Cry me a fucking river!" Tame exclaims. "Christian Porter had the weight of the News Corp press – which is the majority – behind him. Try being a sixteen-year-old who has just reported a serial paedophile to police, and then being called a whore in your hometown. Like, suck it up, Porter."

Michael Bradley, who first met Tame when Marque Lawyers contributed legal support to #LetHerSpeak, notes the essential role of activists like her and Higgins. "The insurgency has immense force," he says. "Because it's got justice, and it's got a more articulate set of spokespeople. It's got heroes, like Grace and Brittany, who are actually bringing a different language to the conversation, because they are not expressing shame. It's got the people who've been fighting this war for a long time, who have the language and the expertise and the evidence to answer every argument that gets thrown up." Bradley says that at his firm, which works closely with rape and sexual assault advocacy organisations, he has already seen many young women seeking advice, supported by the examples of Higgins and Tame. "More and more are making the choice to not just do nothing. I think that's a big change." He doesn't see an end to this movement, because once this ball is rolling, it may never stop. "This society is absolutely full to the brim with survivors. There is this current running under the surface constantly – that, historically, we haven't even noticed, because it's been kept sub-surface. Now it's starting to bubble up in all sorts of random and occasionally seismic ways. There's *so* many. It's endemic, and we know it. That's why it's not going to stop."

MEN

As Morrison "fumbled" the response to Brittany Higgins, "mismanaged" the fury of Australian women, and seemed "overwhelmed" by the crisis engulfing his government, things were actually turning out just fine for the prime minister. No doubt he *was* frustrated by the unrelenting media focus on "women's issues" – a subject that holds no value for him – and was having to work very hard to chart a path out of that. But was his response merely one of clumsiness and ineptitude, as some in the press gallery suggested? Maybe not.

In March, when public rancour was at its highest, Katharine Murphy posited an alternative theory. "Let me share a basic insight about Morrison that you might find useful. This prime minister speaks almost exclusively to one cohort of voters: men at risk of voting Labor."

For me, this was like being handed the Rosetta Stone. With this decoding, we can better deal with the pressing, albeit uncomfortable issue: why his approach may appeal to this cohort of men – "blokes [who are] genuinely dumbfounded about why women are so angry" – and the patient women who love them. As Murphy explains, "patient women" are "inclined to understand rather than judge when men refuse to get obvious things … and respond with nurturing, stoic patience rather than incredulity and fury." With this insight, it becomes possible to imagine how even Morrison's failures may, for this cohort, augment his "daggy dad" persona: the avid rugby league fan who is doing his best to learn the rules of a confusing new world.

Whether Morrison's gambit will pay off in the long run is impossible to say. Male voters certainly remained onside through the worst of it: polling from Essential Media in March 2021 showed that Morrison continued to enjoy a 65 per cent male approval rating throughout the crisis, while approval from women dropped precipitously, from 65 per cent in February to 46 per cent by April. The female vote climbed again, though, to 55 per cent in May, before falling again off the back of the vaccination debacle to

45 per cent in September (with men at 56 per cent). It's impossible to say exactly what feeds into this two-dimensional data, but it seems fair to say that the resurgence of #MeToo was not a mortal threat to Morrison's government (although it may influence the voters in Pearce looking at Christian Porter's name on a ballot next year).

There was a little data point in that Essential poll that gave me the chills. From January to March, Morrison's approval rating among young men aged eighteen to thirty-four *jumped* more than 10 per cent, from 56 per cent to 67 per cent. This may have been "just static" in a small sample, as Katharine Murphy suggested. Alternatively, it may indicate something that requires close attention: is there a backlash against #MeToo fomenting among young men?

*

This is something Laura Bates first noticed as a trend in 2018. As the founder of the Everyday Sexism Project she had for eight years spoken regularly to UK high-school students about sex, respect, consent and equality. She was no stranger to confused and sometimes angry teenagers, but what she saw in those high-school audiences was different. There was "a marked and sinister shift" in the feedback she was getting from some male students, who had obviously come to her talk prepared to undermine her and saw her as a "hate-filled feminazi who wanted to destroy men." She soon realised they were also spouting the same misinformation – false rape allegations are common, most domestic violence victims are men – and were even citing the same baseless statistics. What she learnt from these boys was that their hatred of her was not organic: they were being groomed, indoctrinated and radicalised online in what's known as the "manosphere." In this alternate "red pill" reality, a number of major subcultures – incels, pick-up artists, Men Who Go Their Own Way and men's rights activists – were promoting the same premise: that there is a feminist conspiracy "seeking to destroy the lives of white men, who are the real victims in our society." The boys were all being lured down the same digital rabbit holes:

"well-oiled grooming machines capitalising on algorithms and social media platforms to radicalise young men into hatred of women."

Bates wanted to understand exactly how these boys were being radicalised, so she created an online persona, "Alex," and entered the manosphere. As Alex, Bates travelled through an endless proliferation of networks and groups, whose members and visitors connect through blogs, websites, vlogs, forums and chatrooms such as Reddit, 4chan and 8chan. All told, they host tens of millions of connections between users. Alex had a typical profile: "college-educated, disaffected white man in his early 20s, unlucky in love, and with a sense of discomfort about conversations going on around him about privilege."

Without any real intent, Alex moved easily from "watching funny memes on Instagram, then viral YouTube clips of debates, Facebook groups, gaming livestreams" to generic sites where men were presented as "the real victims." Bates has dedicated her adult life to fighting sexism and misogyny, but it wasn't hard for her to see how this would appeal to young men like Alex. Her online persona was soon learning that "he wasn't a loser, he was an underdog; he wasn't unsuccessful, he was downtrodden." Here was community he couldn't get elsewhere. Jokes about women started out relatively benign, but gradually, as Alex moved through the manosphere, became "more extreme in their misogyny" until, "somewhere along the way, they stopped being jokes." Until the misogyny was normal – and very dark.

The manosphere is a set of distinct subcultures, and its membership among young Australian men is probably not substantial. But its impact is not confined to its membership. Just as the hyper-industrialisation of porn has had a significant influence on mainstream culture, so too does the manosphere seep out of its specific forums and normalise attitudes once considered fringe – or just obviously misogynistic. The popularity of figures such as Canadian academic Jordan Peterson and podcast host Joe Rogan, both of whom have massive followings among young Australian men, is testament to this cultural shift. Peterson has toured here twice, quickly selling out events across Australia. His worldview positions women's empowerment as a threat to natural hierarchies and proposes that the same model of masculinity that civilised the world is now facing an existential threat from feminism. Both Peterson and Rogan are brash personalities, "uncancellable," who provide a model for how men can move around confidently in the world, be successful, and situate themselves in the traditions established by the Greeks. For young men watching feminism advance with unbridled fury, Peterson is a balm for their worry and confusion. He tells it straight: anything that can be cast as "feminine," even climate change activism, is an existential threat to the grand tradition of patriarchy: "Most of the global warming posturing is a masquerade for anti-capitalists to have a go at the Western patriarchy," he told *Good Weekend* in 2018, "you can't trust the data because there is too much ideology involved." Faced with a choice between this and what #MeToo is asking – for men to take responsibility, be accountable and relinquish enough power to allow women greater equality – it's not hard to see why many young men are choosing option A.

The conundrum we now face is that the very power of #MeToo – which has employed methods of public shaming to out not just perpetrators, but also men whose remarks reveal a vintage attitude towards women – may be alienating some men and boys, and even making them more susceptible to the manosphere.

Richie Hardcore, a New Zealand–based educator and former Muay Thai champion, spends his days trying to turn boys away from this kind of misogyny. He is an energetic supporter of #MeToo. But what he's noticed in some boys is that they feel as though #MeToo has come to define being a man as a problem – no matter how one behaves. The young men he educates typically don't distinguish between the term "masculinity" and "the biological reality of being a male." So when they hear terms like "toxic masculinity," they hear that *men* are toxic. "When you spell it out for men, they get it."

"I spoke at a construction site the other day and I was like, 'Yo, who's angry all the time and doesn't know what to do with it?' And they were like, 'Yo, me too.' And I went, 'Man, when I was young, I used to punch holes in walls. My positive pathway was sport, martial arts, all these tattoos and muscles and kickboxing titles, but that didn't take the pain away. I still hurt no matter how much of a 'real man' I was. It took me, like, crying and going to a therapist's office to ask for help, and taking my mask off, to help me be a healthy man. You know, our idea of masculinity doesn't work for us bros, right?'" Hardcore says this resonated straightaway, and after the session he had "a queue of men – literally, a queue" coming up to him and asking for help. "One said, 'Man, I never hit my missus' – that's his language, not mine – 'but I smashed up my house, and I hate it. I hate being like this and I don't know what to do.'" Hardcore says the problem is the scarcity of help available for such men. "We need to break down the patriarchy," he says. "But we need the right fucking tools for the job, you know? Empathy is a wonderful, wonderful teaching tool in a way that shame isn't."

Hardcore is aware that even asking for care around how we speak to men about sexism, misogyny and violence may draw criticism that he is somehow excusing these things or sympathising with sexist men. But what he's interested in, more than being palatable, is connecting with boys and men who may otherwise be drawn further into misogyny. The challenge Hardcore names is a tough one, but what use is being "right" if we end up alienating the very men we want to listen to us, and change?

*

Why is hatred of and contempt for women still a default position for so many boys and men? What happens to those vulnerable, loving little boys that sees them grow up to be perpetrators of sexual violence, abuse and harassment?

Aside from factors such as childhood abuse and neglect, which can be significant in the lives of perpetrators, the emergence into maleness is a form of trauma in itself – a "normal traumatisation" experienced by *all* boys, when they learn that it's not safe to be emotional, expressive, vulnerable. American family therapist Terry Real says boys begin to experience this kind of "patriarchal" trauma when they're really young – around three or four. "Before our boys have learnt to read," he tells me, "they have already read the code of masculinity." At this vulnerable stage, boys learn to be contemptuous of those "unsafe" feminine traits – particularly their own. Being a boy means *not* being a girl. To be a "boy" means learning to separate from your feelings, from your fears and vulnerabilities, and put on a strong face. "There's research that indicates that boys are less expressive at three, four, five," says Real. "It doesn't mean they feel less, but they've already figured out it's not politic to let people know what you feel. Three, four or five. That's a hell of a trauma."

Having learnt to separate himself from "feminine" traits, the growing boy is tasked with turning "the vice of lack of feeling and connection into the virtue of being a strong man." This type of masculinity requires boys to remain hypervigilant against strong emotions; they must remain in control. When they fail to do this, they may be shamed for it – by their friends, peers or parents. My husband, David Hollier, who co-wrote this chapter, is a psychotherapist who sees many grown men dealing with the long-term fallout of this "normal trauma" from their childhood. One of his male clients, whom we'll call "Simon," permitted us to share one of his formative experiences. Simon was eleven years old and had played poorly in his Saturday Aussie Rules game. Afterwards, he made a joke about it to his coach, in front of players and other parents. He wasn't really worried about the game he'd just played, because he was excited to be going with his dad to see a big rugby match later. But once he was alone with his father in the car, his father turned on him, screaming at him for joking about a performance that had let his whole team down. It went on and on, and by the end of it Simon had decided that he would never again let anyone see him with his guard down.

In the rites of patriarchal masculinity, the kind of shame Simon experienced becomes a tool for reinscribing the need to stay in control, because the memory of losing it invokes a feeling that is searingly painful. Experiences like this deposit in many boys an extreme sensitivity to threats of shame. The longer that goes unacknowledged, the more harm it creates, until any perceived threat must immediately be extinguished. Much of the behaviour we might describe as "toxic" arises as a defence against shame – the greater the shame, the more urgent the defence – and there is no greater defence against shame than grandiosity and narcissism. Once this defence is established, the feminine – externally, and internally – is designated as threatening. The easiest way to extinguish that threat is to objectify the feminine and hold it in contempt.

For psychologist Niobe Way, this is all very simple. "We essentially raise boys in a culture that asks them to disconnect from their core humanity, and tell them that if you are emotional, relational, then you're not a man," she told NPR two days after #MeToo went viral. Worse still, she said, our culture exalts the men who best succeed at disconnecting – the lonely and aggressive ones – and puts them in positions of power. Little wonder we still have such high rates of sexual violence, harassment and domestic abuse. "If you raise boys to go against their nature, some of them will grow up and act crazy."

Obviously, a solid proportion of boys are not shamed by their parents when they get emotionally overwhelmed, or struggle to cope with failure or defeat – and they learn healthy tolerance of a range of feelings. Regardless of their upbringing, however, all boys will at some point find themselves as men positioned along a spectrum of traditional masculinity – alphas at one end, and on down the line until they're tagged with the labels of femininity, from "pussy" to "gay," soft, or simply "girl." Those on the low end of the spectrum become vulnerable – as we saw in Respect@ Work, it is men who don't conform to standard norms of masculinity who are most likely to become targets of workplace sexual harassment, most commonly at the hands of multiple male harassers.

By adolescence, boys arrive at a conundrum: girls, who bear the feminine traits they have been taught to exclude, are now seen to be desirable. Few boys navigate this passage unscarred; fewer still do so with any realistic guidance from adults. We are a society deeply and mysteriously afraid of sex education, and into this vacuum the multi-billion-dollar porn industry directs a never-ending stream of hardcore pornography. As boys reach adolescence, most will be consuming a diet of porn in which, generally speaking, there is no gauging of consent, no real intimacy, and the clear message is that no matter what men do to them, the women will love it.

Governments, schools, community leaders and "champions of change" might promote messages of equality and respect, but almost nobody is talking about this elephant in the room. Meanwhile, teenage boys are climaxing daily to freely available misogynistic pornography. Is it any wonder these boys grow up feeling that they can get away with saying one thing, while doing another?

*

Perhaps the strongest cultural touchstone for this doublethink is the Australian virtue of "mateship." If the central demand of #MeToo is accountability, it's hard to imagine a more powerful form of kryptonite than this treasured identity.

No Australian needs reminding of the sacred place accorded to mateship in our national mythology. Whether you picture a digger, a bronzed surfer, footy players celebrating victory, firefighters facing the blaze – all Australians are raised to understand instinctively the virtues mateship embodies: good humour, honour, commitment, loyalty, resilience. That's the flag-waving version. In reality, the central elements of mateship are more telling. Mates are men; they are tough and emotionally reserved; they rip into each other with jokes and put-downs; they crow about sexual conquests and talk shit about women without fear of being told off. The rules are clear: no obvious caring and little to no touching. In other words, nothing "gay." If you stick to the code of mateship, a mate will always support you. No matter what. Loyalty to your mate is a higher virtue than observance of any law. As Professor Bob Pease from Deakin University explains, this is unique to Australia, dating back to the early days of colonisation, when the Europeans taking over Indigenous territory were living in harsh conditions, and often without women. "All patriarchal societies have forms of male bonding," he tells me, "but there's something about the Australian form of mateship that exalts it to a higher degree."

Since John Howard demanded, during the 1997 referendum, that mateship be included in the preamble to the new constitution if Australia voted for a Republic (which he opposed), it has been positioned as a value for "mainstream Australians," and one that must be protected from the "anti-mate" elites. The conscription of mateship into the culture wars has rendered discussion of this complex national identity defensive and brittle.

But the thing #MeToo demands we confront is that mateship isn't just about loyalty; it is also about protection, impunity and, following its perpetration, the erasure of sexual violence. Bruce Baer Arnold of the University of Canberra has written persuasively on the links between mateship, sexual violence and secrecy. Using a series of Australian films (*Wake in Fright*, *The Chant of Jimmie Blacksmith*, *Mad Max* and *Ghosts . . . of the Civil Dead*), Arnold traces a version of mateship where male bystanders and witnesses of sexual violence are compelled to silence. He argues that this goes beyond secrecy – it is a need to erase the violence altogether.

Few events in Australia's modern history more starkly illustrate the erasure of sexual violence than the rape and murder of Leigh Leigh in Stockton, near Newcastle, in 1989. Indeed, the facts of this case took years to emerge, and did so only after a series of reviews and investigations driven by a few local residents and the formidable advocacy of Kerry Carrington.

Fourteen-year-old Leigh was at her first party, when she was almost carried away from the venue by one of the boys, who would become known as NC1, and sexually assaulted. When she returned, the young Leigh was drunk, distressed and bleeding between her legs. She tried to get someone to help her. Nineteen-year-old Guy Wilson – the oldest boy at the party – instead asked her for sex. When she refused, he and about ten other boys kicked, spat at and poured beer on Leigh. Shortly afterwards, Leigh was seen staggering away from the party.

Her body was found the following morning. The autopsy would show the cause of death as a fractured skull and brain damage, and there was evidence of multiple injuries, choking and violent sexual assault.

Not one of the boys was ever charged with sexual assault. The guy charged with Leigh's murder, Matthew Webster, was presented at the trial as a "gentle giant," despite being known in the community as a "thug." Even the psychologist's report for the court presented Webster's view that he killed Leigh because, having rejected his advances, "she became the living proof that even a slut, a property of the clan, thought he was not good enough to have sex with."

Through the trial and its various reviews, Leigh herself was – in the community and the media (most egregiously in *The Newcastle Herald*) – effectively put on trial for her appearance, her intoxication and even the conversations she'd had with her mother about sex. Leigh's loved ones were left to negotiate the chasm between the post-mortem and the "facts" as established by the justice system.

Among those called on to bring justice to Leigh and her family, we see a disturbing and insidious network of collusion, secret deals, incompetence, rule breaches and misuse of laws. Over more than a decade, the bodies tasked with revealing the truth and bringing justice fell into line to conceal the horrific sexual violence perpetrated on a fourteen-year-old girl attending her first party. The case was so riddled with errors, improper deals with those involved and abdication of duty that, eleven years later, a review by the Police Integrity Commission (one of eight reviews into the trial) recommended that the lead investigator be sacked for "gross dereliction of duty" and that five officers be criminally charged.

*

The loyalty code of mateship is not just used to erase sexual violence, but also invoked against men who dare to step outside it. ABC journalist Mark Willacy has been dogged in exposing how this order of secrecy is being abused within the Australian military to conceal alleged war crimes. Speaking to Richard Fidler on *Conversations*, Willacy recounted the story of an SAS operator, "Tom," who witnessed the unlawful killing of an innocent, disabled Afghan man, who was then dressed in a weapons magazine to make him look like a combatant. At the debrief that followed back at base, the soldier responsible was praised for taking out a high-value target. Tom, says Willacy, then "did something that was totally unthinkable in the SAS patrol dynamics. He got up and he walked out and said, 'I'm not going to be part of this bullshit.'"

This "unthinkable" act triggered the standard defence required by mateship. As Bruce Baer Arnold describes, this defence "situates the toughest, roughest, most emotionally distant and most aggressive man as the one most deserving of respect and worthy of emulation. That man will on occasion be the most disturbed man among his peers, prepared to unthinkingly enforce his will and impose his desires on mates." It was this man Tom had just challenged, breaking the code of mateship by putting the truth before his loyalty to the group.

For merely refusing to valorise this man, Tom's "career eventually was ruined, he was brutalised [by fellow SAS members], his mental health suffered." Such were the "consequences for decent people in the SAS … who tried to take a stand or were uncomfortable with the cover-up," says Willacy. "They suffered greatly." Willacy himself has been viciously attacked for undermining the reputation of our military, even labelled a traitor.

As we ask men to join as allies and to call out sexist and dangerous behaviour, we must give careful thought to what this can cost them. However obvious it seems, however reasonable it is to demand it, the fact remains that men who openly resist sexist and abusive men can find themselves in perilous positions. A big question for #MeToo, then, becomes: how do we convince men they'll be supported if they resist and overcome sexist masculinity?

*

The subject of "men" – how they've responded to #MeToo, how women want them to change, the unfairness of trial by media – has consumed a lot of column inches since 2017. Of course, just as it's foolish to essentialise "women" (though I'm surely guilty of that in parts of this essay), it's similarly inaccurate to reduce 3.9 billion men to one homogenous category, especially when attempting to analyse particular responses, behaviours and beliefs. It doesn't account for people who are non-binary, for starters, but even if we're just talking about cis men, it creates more questions than it answers. Which men? All men? Some men more than others? White men? #NotAllMen? I'm not going to pretend to capture here what men – Australian men, migrant men, groups of men – think about #MeToo, nor can I distil their "response" into a neat package. But I have attempted to engage with the various ways this movement is reaching them, and why it's not.

The basic requests of the #MeToo movement are simple. To men, it says: *Stop harassing, abusing and raping us. Stop objectifying us. Stop coercing us.* So far, so good. But when it comes to engaging men on these issues – or having them step up as allies – it gets more complicated. What right do men have to talk about #MeToo? Do we as women really want them in this conversation? Should we only accept men with spotless records as allies? Can we trust heterosexual men to speak honestly, and not just use the movement as cover? Do we, ultimately, believe it's possible for them to change?

*

As I was finishing this essay, Josh Bornstein sent me a single-line email: "What do you reckon? Are we winning?"

I think, unequivocally, #MeToo has changed Australia. In one industry after the next, the reckoning has gathered force: just this year, we've seen it arrive in the music industry, with some of Australia's most senior and previously untouchable music industry figures, Sony Music's Tony Glover and, most remarkably, industry legend Denis Handlin, sacked for bullying and harassment. The mining industry, too, has taken the first steps towards addressing sexual harassment, bullying and rape – admitting that it actually has a problem.

This reckoning is not just changing internal cultures within certain industries; it is changing the way certain industries influence our culture at large. It's no coincidence that, here and overseas, #MeToo landed so powerfully in two fields: entertainment and the judiciary. They were spotlighted not simply because we give priority to the trauma of privileged women (though of course we do), but because predatory attitudes in Hollywood and the law affect *all* of us. These are two of the most influential parts of our culture: one establishes dominant cultural narratives and the other decides what is socially permissible. In fact, I'd argue that the focus on these industries was not driven so much by a concern for the women affected, but more for the integrity of the institutions they worked for. There's no doubt that more focus needs to be put on predatory men in less glamorous industries – in every industry – and that the safety of *all* women must be our priority. However, we shouldn't understate the importance of exposing predatory male behaviour in these areas – particularly the Australian judicial system. With the Dyson Heydon inquiry, #MeToo has given us a shot at finally putting the broom through institutions that have systematically disbelieved and victim-blamed women and children for centuries. These predatory men – and those committed to protecting them – are presiding over matters of domestic and sexual violence, as well as sexual harassment. They decide whether a story is plausible or whether it meets the test of "reasonable doubt." The stark truth that now faces all of us is that a percentage of the men who disbelieve and dismiss victims in their courtrooms may be engaging in predatory behaviour themselves. Many may have supposed that in the past – but now the proof is building that such behaviour is rife and systemic. We have to assess #MeToo from this higher vantage point: instead of staying at ground level and focusing on each high-profile predator and his victims, we need to zoom out to see how exposing that predatory behaviour may catalyse cultural change that will, in fact, benefit all of us.

But #MeToo's ability to sustain itself will depend on the nous of its exponents. Change will not happen simply because it *should*, or because it's *worthy*. The work cannot be pushed through with blunt force – it has to be strategic. There are few shrewder minds in this area than Nina Funnell, whose #LetHerSpeak campaign was, in many ways, the most organised and tactical #MeToo movement in Australia. Survivor-led, with a clear objective to change laws and to educate, #LetHerSpeak was not, however, packaged as a movement against sexual violence. "The reason it worked, and caught fire the way it did, is because I was repackaging the issue of sexual assault and framing it through a freedom of speech lens. Which meant that conservatives, who ordinarily would resist any kind of messaging around violence against women, were suddenly being engaged as well." Funnell did not just expect this audience to eat their vegetables – she cooked the meal in a way that would appeal to them. She partnered with News Corp, a media organisation generally antagonistic to the feminist agenda. "If you go and look at all of the articles I did with people, once they got their court orders – in all of them, I'm usually unpacking other issues around sexual violence, like victim-blaming attitudes, rape myths, the best ways of responding to disclosure, sexual assault within regional communities." In Tasmania, the campaign had a 92 per cent approval rating, "which is unheard of."

On this strategic front, it may have been a blessing in disguise that #MeToo claimed fewer high-profile scalps in Australia than the United States. We are, as *The New York Times* describes, "a secretive, proudly masculine culture" which "shrouds law enforcement and the courts in unusual secrecy, particularly in cases of sexual and family violence." Defamation laws are a symptom of this secretive culture: one in which perpetrators of sexual violence are protected not only by power and the justice system, but by their "mates." I think that if we had seen dozens of well-loved national figures exposed as sexual predators – even just a per capita equivalent of the hundreds exposed in the United States – the backlash may have been so severe that, and the level of change so threatening, that it may have extinguished the movement altogether. When I put this point to Funnell, she agrees: "I don't think we had the community readiness for something like that to happen."

Besides, although it's important to hold powerful men accountable, outing them one-by-one is not the end game. High-profile scalps are the "sizzle" – like the cutting-edge outfits you put in a fashion store window. One of those outfits might sell, but its primary purpose is to get customers into the shop so they will buy the basic T-shirts hanging on the racks. Now, don't get me wrong: high-profile scalps are the backbone of #MeToo.

Taken properly, they can bring renewed energy to the movement, trigger wake-up calls in industries and, importantly, expose dangerous predators and stop them abusing with impunity. But, as journalist and author Susan Faludi explains, we cannot get too fixated on individuals. "Fighting the patriarch and fighting the patriarchy are also distinct – and the former tends to be more popular than the latter. It's easier to mobilize against a demon, as every military propagandist – and populist demagogue – knows. It's harder, and less electrifying, to forge the terms of peace. Declaring war is thrilling. Nation-building isn't."

But I haven't yet answered Bornstein's question: *Are we winning?*

My sense is that while we may not be winning all the battles – and we're suffering badly in some – we *are* winning the war. But this is not a war with a clear end in sight. A century from now, women will be holding signs – just as they did at the March 4 Justice – that say, "I can't believe we're still protesting this shit." I was in Chicago when Barack Obama was elected president in 2008, and I remember the euphoric commentary of the following days and weeks – that America was now a "post-racial" society. I was in the Middle East for the tail end of the Arab uprisings, at a time when so many believed that power was finally being taken back by the people, that tyrants were on borrowed time and that social media would liberate us all. When you are seeing the unthinkable happen before your eyes, it is very tempting to get caught up in the moment and see the job as done. But the job will never be done. Social change is a long game of snakes and ladders – you go forwards, you go backwards, but most importantly you keep playing. I think our collective consciousness is as high as it's ever been on issues of gender, race and democracy. The question that #MeToo is raising is a deeply human question about power and violence, and how societies manage that. The battle to keep that question in the public mind is unceasing; the darkening weather on climate change, surveillance, white supremacy, capitalism and corruption is generating its own dangerous fire conditions that will make this fight harder yet. There is no utopia waiting for us. We make the gains while we can, we celebrate the advances, and then we get back to work.

ACKNOWLEDGMENTS AND SOURCES

Thank you to Kristine Ziwica for her research, and David Hollier for his editorial contribution to "Men."

1 "shocked", "disgusted"; "shameful", etc.: Scott Morrison, Press conference, Australian Parliament House, Canberra, ACT, 23 March 2021.
2 "Just so": Luke Pearson, Twitter, 23 March 2021, https://twitter.com/lukelpearson/status/1374162199569076227?lang=en, accessed 1 November 2021.
3 a disagreement about press gallery politics: Sean Kelly, *The Game*, Black Inc., Carlton, 2021, p. 223.
5 "Actually, Prime Minister": Laura Tingle, 7.30, ABC TV, 23 March 2021.
6 "Social media is not a safe space": Emma Brockes, "#MeToo founder Tarana Burke: 'You have to use your privilege to serve other people'", *The Guardian*, 15 January 2018.
6 "If you've been sexually harassed": Alyssa Milano, Twitter, 16 October 2017, https://twitter.com/Alyssa_Milano/status/919659438700670976, accessed 1 November 2021.
6 "I wrote a summary": Louise Allan, Twitter, 28 September 2021, https://twitter.com/louisejallan/status/1442675831524847623, accessed 8 November 2021.
6–7 "I was suddenly aware": Sophia Rose O'Rourke, Twitter, 28 September 2021, https://twitter.com/Auntie_Sophie/status/1442832639442837505, accessed 8 November 2021.
7 "I remember": Tim Baker, Twitter, 28 September 2021, https://twitter.com/bytimbaker/status/1442682889661915145, accessed 11 November 2021.
7 "like the Berlin Wall coming down": Jane Campion, quoted in Catherine Shoard, "Jane Campion: #MeToo felt like 'end of apartheid' for women", *Guardian Australia*, 2 September 2021.
7 "purge" and "Spontaneously": Megan O'Neill, Twitter, 28 September 2021, https://twitter.com/megansallesi/status/1442778026379386887, accessed 8 November 2021.
7–8 "I felt like I wasn't lonely", "It made my anger", "I didn't really understand #MeToo": Comments on Instagram, 28 September 2021, www.instagram.com/p/CUWVwdah4Qr, accessed 8 November 2021.
8 "I started thinking": Aileen Marwung Walsh, Twitter, 28 September 2021, https://twitter.com/aileenwalsh16/status/1442716554051817472, accessed 11 November 2021.

9	"It has been amazing": Tarana Burke, Instagram, 16 October 2017, www.instagram.com/p/BaSTg9Rg47G/?hl=en, accessed 11 November 2021.
10	"The protective cladding": Kristine Ziwica, "'I can't help it I'm a dinosaur': Let's bust the sexual predator excuses for real solutions", *Women's Agenda*, 15 October 2017.
12	The *Globe*'s reporting: It continues to unfold to this day; in October this year, a new report revealed that French clergy sexually abused around 216,000 children over the past seventy years.
12	"a shaking of the foundations", "In an earlier era": Rebecca Solnit, *Men Explain Things to Me and Other Essays*, Haymarket, Chicago, 2015.
12	"predatory behaviour": Steven Erlanger and Katrin Bennhold, "Soul-searching in France after official's arrest jolts nation", *The New York Times*, 15 May 2011.
13	"boys, girls, men and women": "BBC star Jimmy Savile 'committed sex acts on dead bodies' while volunteering at hospital", ABC (online), 26 June 2014.
13	"transformed how we deal", "We reassessed", "the BBC": Jonathan Maitland, "Jimmy Savile: 10 years on, what has changed in uncovering abuse?", *The Guardian*, 1 August 2021.
13	"gutted and dismayed", "it's important", "It's just sad": "Rolf Harris guilty of all assault charges (update)", *RN Breakfast*, ABC Radio, 1 July 2014.
14	"You don't want": Joe Biden, "Joe Biden to Colleges: 'Step Up. It's Time'", *Time*, 15 May 2014.
14	"The girls don't flock": Elliot Rodgers, "My Twisted World", www.documentcloud.org/documents/1173808-elliot-rodger-manifesto.html, accessed 1 November 2021
15	"forcing himself", "seeing semen": Noreen Malone and Amanda Demme, "'I'm no longer afraid': 35 women tell their stories about being assaulted by Bill Cosby, and the culture that wouldn't listen", *The Cut*, 27 July 2015.
16	"You don't know me": Kate J.M. Baker, "Here's the powerful letter the Stanford victim read to her attacker", *BuzzFeed*, 3 June 2016.
16	"she is radically rewriting": Nina Funnell, "Don't ask me to feel sorry for my rapist", *The Daily Telegraph*, 10 June 2016.
16	"20 minutes of action": Dan A. Turner, "'A steep price to pay for 20 minutes of action': Dad defends Stanford sex offender", *The Washington Post*, 6 June 2016.
17	"Turner's sense of entitlement": Kasey Edwards, "Stanford earns a PhD in cluelessness for its woeful Brock Turner response", *The Sydney Morning Herald*, 26 August 2016.
17	"by the pussy": "Transcript: Donald Trump's taped comments about women", *The New York Times*, 8 October 2016.

17   "when the *Access Hollywood* tape dropped", "quite possibly": Maureen Ryan, "The Access Hollywood tape was vile – and maybe, a vital tipping point", *Vanity Fair*, 7 October 2020.

18   "ugly underbelly of persistent sexism": Lydia Feng and Kelsey Munro, "Why Trump is good for the women's movement", SBS (online), 7 March 2018.

18   "Trump has reinvigorated feminism": Jodi Enda, quoted in Elizabeth Blair, "Women are speaking up about harassment and abuse, but why now?", NPR (online), 27 October 2017.

20   "omnipotent male perpetrators": "Not just pretty faces, they have powerful voices too: Celebrity discourse and the #MeToo movement", *Europe Now*, 10 March 2020.

20   "Currently, I am investigating": Tracey Spicer, Twitter, 18 October 2017, https://twitter.com/traceyspicer/status/920402701124431872?lang=en, accessed 8 November 2021.

20   "Australian men", "and how rare": Richard Guilliatt, "Tracey Spicer, NOW Australia and the gathering storm", *The Australian*, 7 August 2018.

21   "a 'psychotic bully'", "I've been trying to think": Kate McClymont, "'A high-grade, twisted abuser': Don Burke a sexual harasser and bully, claims series of women", *The Sydney Morning Herald*, 26 November 2017.

21   "every single person in management": Kate McClymont, "'A high-grade, twisted abuser': Don Burke a sexual harasser and bully, claims series of women", *The Sydney Morning Herald*, 26 November 2017.

22   *New Matilda* exposé: Nina Funnell and Chris Graham, "'My beautiful penis': More women come forward to expose barrister Charles Waterstreet", *New Matilda*, 31 October 2017.

23   "oppressive and notoriously complex": Louisa Lim, "How Australia became the defamation capital of the world", *The New York Times*, 5 March 2019.

23   "If it wasn't for journalists": Michael Cameron, quoted in Jenna Price, "Wondering what happened to #metoo? Women are too frightened to speak", *The Sydney Morning Herald*, 3 May 2018.

24   "monstrous", "We can't get caught up": Tarana Burke, 2019 City of Sydney Peace Prize Lecture, Sydney Peace Foundation, https://youtu.be/2d4LMhTJYbg, accessed 3 November 2021.

25   "This is not a movement": Jane Wakefield, "MeToo founder Tarana Burke: Campaign now 'unrecognisable'", BBC (online), 29 November 2018.

25   "unrecognisable", "My vision": "Propelled by possibility: Tarana Burke speaks at TEDWomen 2018", *TEDblog*, 29 November 2018, https://blog.ted.com/propelled-by-possibility-tarana-burke-speaks-at-tedwomen-2018, accessed

8 November 2021.

26   "People ask": Jodi Kantor, "Tarana Burke talks about the surprising origins of #MeToo", *The New York Times*, 10 September 2021.

27   "Men and women", etc.: "What did #MeToo really achieve", *The Inquiry* (podcast), 20 December 2018.

28   "glaringly white and middle-class", etc.: Hannah Ryan and Gina Rushton, "The leaders of Australia's 'Time's Up' movement made big promises they couldn't keep", *Buzzfeed*, 18 October 2019.

30   "through therapy": Jane Wakefield, "MeToo found Tarana Burke campaign now 'unrecognisable'", *Buzzfeed*, 29 November 2018.

31   "whingeing", "if you spread": Nick Miller, "Germaine Greer challenges #MeToo campaign", *The Sydney Morning Herald*, 21 January 2018.

32   "witch hunt" letter: "Nous défendons une liberté d'importuner, indispensable à la liberté sexuelle", *Le Monde*, 9 January 2018.

32   "women could solve", "serious intellectual rift", etc.: Moira Donegan, "How #MeToo revealed the central rift within feminism today", *The Guardian*, 11 May 2018.

33   "for many black women": Dr Tess Ryan, "For Indigenous women, the #MeToo movement is a deeper fight against racism, power and oppression", *The Conversation*, 28 October 2019.

34   "Until now": David Leser, "Women, men and the whole damn thing", *The Sydney Morning Herald*, 9 February 2018.

40–41   "A lot of men": Jessica Valenti, quoted in Candice Chung, "Why the Aziz Ansari debate is the conversation we need to have", SBS (online), 16 January 2018.

41   "I'm still not sure", etc.: Anonymous, "I thought I was one of the good guys. Then I read the Aziz Ansari story", *Vox*, 24 January 2018.

42   "You probably did": Toby, "After #MeToo" (podcast), UTS.

42   "It's a terrifying thing to talk about": Jesse David Fox, "Aziz Ansari reflects on sexual-misconduct allegation at his NYC pop-up show", *Vulture*, 12 February 2019.

43–44   "one of the most frightening": Leigh Sales, Peter McCutcheon and Callum Denness, "'I didn't sleep for a week': Catherine Marriott speaks out about alleged sexual harassment by Barnaby Joyce", ABC (online), 18 September 2018.

44   "This impact": Ashleigh Raper, "ABC journalist Ashleigh Raper's statement in full", ABC (online), 8 November 2018.

45   "dined together": Stephen Mayne, "Mayne: All signs point to an early exit for alleged sexual harasser Robert Doyle", *Crikey*, 15 January 2018.

47   "pretty young colleagues", etc.: Clay Lucas and Miki Perkins, "Councillors knew of claims about Doyle – and Faine had an inkling too", *The Age*, 7 February 2018.

47	Garner letter: Helen Garner, "Calling men to account", *The Age*, 10 February 2018.
47	"a lynch mob mentality", etc.: James Oaten, "Robert Doyle victim of 'political witch-hunt': former premier Jeff Kennett", ABC (online), 5 February 2018.
49	"very significant": Ben Rimmer, *Update on the investigation into allegations against the former Lord Mayor, Robert Doyle*, Management report to Council, 13 March 2018, p. 10, par. 11.
49	"misunderstandings", etc.: Emma Page-Campbell, Media statement, https://d3n8a8pro7vhmx.cloudfront.net/gx/pages/2302/attachments/original/1520982962/Emma_Page-Campbell_statement.pdf?1520982962, accessed 4 November 2021.
49	"Sexual predators": Stephen Mayne, "Doyle is finished, but what about the men who supported him?", *Crikey*, 14 March 2018.
51	"I had to do something", etc.: John Howard, "Guns", *Insight*, SBS TV, 2016.
51–52	"I think I am": Malcolm Turnbull, Interview – "Speaking for Myself", 1988, SBS (online), 16 September 2015.
52	"Disrespecting women": Malcolm Turnbull, Remarks to 2016 International Women's Day Parliamentary Breakfast, 3 March 2016.
52	"It is my dream": Turnbull, Press conference to announce $100-million safety package to stop the violence, 24 September 2015.
52	"We finally": Rosie Batty quoted in Judith Ireland, "Malcolm Turnbull's scathing attack on men who commit domestic violence", *The Sydney Morning Herald*, 24 September 2015.
53	"The hypocrisy made me sick": Malcolm Turnbull, *A Bigger Picture*, Hardie Grant, Richmond, 2020.
53	"unequivocal assurance": Louise Yaxley, "Malcolm Turnbull bans ministers from sex with staffers, but resists calls to ask Barnaby Joyce to resign", ABC (online), 15 February 2018.
53	"I don't care": Malcolm Turnbull, Press conference, Parliament House, Canberra, ACT, 15 February 2018.
54	"The idea": Eryk Bagshaw, "Minister for Women Kelly O'Dwyer sounds warning over 'me too' movement", *The Sydney Morning Herald*, 6 March 2018.
54	"disgraceful and sexist", etc.: Adam Gartrell, "Michaelia Cash forced to withdraw 'disgraceful and sexist' comments about Bill Shorten's staff", *The Sydney Morning Herald*, 28 February 2018.
54	"no hesitation": Georgie Dent, "Finally! A minister for women who is a feminist & willing to fight for change", *Women's Agenda*, 6 March 2018.
57	one in five: Australian Human Rights Commission, "Chapter 3: The extent of

sexual harassment in Australia", in *Sexual Harassment: Serious business, Results of the 2008 sexual harassment phone survey*, AHRC, October 2008.

57 one in three: Australian Human Rights Commission, *Respect@Work: Sexual Harassment National Inquiry Report (2020)*, AHRC, 5 March 2020.

58 sexually assaulted in a university setting: including travel to and from campus.

58 1.6 per cent: Australian Human Rights Commission, "Executive summary", *National University Student Survey on Sexual Assault and Sexual Harassment*, https://humanrights.gov.au/our-work/executive-summary-8, accessed 8 November 2021.

60 "a long and widespread reputation": Michael Balter, "From Oxford to Adelaide: Ancient DNA expert Alan Cooper's bullying and harassment has left a trail of psychological damage and wrecked careers", *Balter's Blog*, 3 July 2019.

62 "She wanted it": Nina Funnell, "#LetHerSpeak: 'Monster hiding in plain sight' – Grace Tame's sexual abuse ordeal revealed", News.com.au, 22 August 2019.

63 "the culture of enabling abuse": Grace Tame to Michael Bradley, Marque Lawyers, Instagram Live, 5 October 2021, www.instagram.com/tv/CUoS332gc_G, accessed 11 November 2021.

63 "judging from the emails": Richard Baines, "Former private school teacher Nicolaas Bester jailed after calling sexual relationship with student 'awesome'", ABC (online), 12 January 2016.

63 "with great care": Rhiannon Shine, "University students petition against sex offender Nicolaas Bester's presence on campus", ABC (online), 16 May 2017.

63 End Rape on Campus, *The Red Zone Report*, 2018, www.endrapeoncampusau.org, accessed 9 November 2021.

63 "Rathjen was instrumental": Michael Balter, "Peter Rathjen: Serial sexual predator, pedophile protector, and manifestation of all that is rotten at the University of Adelaide?", *Balter's Blog*, 20 May 2020.

64 "We believe": Natalie Whiting, "UTAS student speaks up about her sexual assault to help other victims feel validated", ABC (online), 2 August 2017.

65 "last straw", etc.: David Crowe, "'The last straw': Furious MP Julia Banks to quit parliament over the axing of Malcolm Turnbull", *The Sydney Morning Herald*, 29 August 2018.

65 "Often when": "Julia Banks' full statement to the House of Representatives", *The Sydney Morning Herald*, 27 November 2018.

65 "menacing, controlling wallpaper": Julia Banks, *Power Play: Breaking through bias, barriers and boys' clubs*, Hardie Grant, Richmond, 2021.

66 "thrilled", "Oh Boy": Alex Mckinnon, "Bettina Arndt's 'fake rape' campaign", *The Saturday Paper*, 29 September 2019.

67	"so-called sex offender": Bettina Arndt, "Feminists persecute disgraced teacher", YouTube, 15 December 2017, https://youtu.be/CVqkV-HJOOY, accessed 8 November 2021.
67	"over the years", "young girls": Bettina Arndt, "Feminists persecute disgraced teacher", YouTube, 15 December 2017, https://youtu.be/CVqkV-HJOOY, accessed 8 November 2021.
70	"Mr Sippel's conduct": *Golding v. Sippel and The Laundry Chute Pty Ltd* [2021] ICQ 14.
72	"Those who think": Kieran Pender, Madeleine Castles and Tom Hvala, "Courting progress", *The Monthly*, 15 March 2021.
73	"take a leading role" and subsequent testimonies: Australian Human Rights Commission, *Respect@Work: Sexual Harassment National Inquiry Report*, AHRC, 2020.
73	2018 Australian Human Rights Commission survey: Australian Human Rights Commission, *Everyone's Business: 2018 Sexual Harassment Survey*, AHRC, 2020.
74	"a common, ongoing and habitual culture of harassment": Kristine Ziwica, "What sparked #MeToo's momentum? Women speaking out en masse", *Women's Agenda*, 18 October 2018.
75	"These women have been groomed": Australian Human Rights Commission, Respect@Work: Sexual Harassment National Inquiry Report, AHRC, 2020.
76	"[H]arassment is not always": Vicki Schultz, "Open Statement on sexual harassment from employment discrimination law scholars", *Stanford Law Review*, vol. 17, June 2018.
80	"small potatoes": Elizabeth C. Tippett, "#MeToo movement finds an unlikely champion in Wall Street, with the new 'Weinstein clause'", *The Conversation*, 3 August 2018.
81	International Bar Association: There's no question that Australians have a higher awareness of what constitutes sexual harassment than, say, Russians. Russian law does not define it, and a quarter of Russian women consider workplace harassment to be a personal matter. So when Russia reports a lower rate of harassment than Australia, it's fair to presume the actual rate may be higher – and the IBA report made that point explicitly. Ranking Australia against Norway, we find that bullying affected over 19 per cent of Norwegian respondents, compared to 61.2 per cent of Australians. On sexual harassment, Norway reported 19.6 per cent, compared to 29.6 per cent for Australia. However, when female respondents were singled out, the Australian figure jumped to 47 per cent – on par with African nations.
81	"wasn't enough": Natassia Chrysanthos, "'The stakes are so high': Inside the two-year Heydon investigation", *The Sydney Morning Herald*, 25 June 2020.

83 "few terse paragraphs": Rachel Doyle, *Power and Consent: In the national interest*, Monash University Publishing, Clayton, 2021.

83 "I have no doubt": Jacqueline Maley and Kate McClymont, "Two High Court judges 'knew of complaints against Dyson Heydon'", *The Sydney Morning Herald*, 25 June 2020.

86 "sharp intelligence", etc.: Louise Milligan, "Friends of woman who accused Cabinet Minister of rape call for inquiry into allegation", ABC (online), 1 March 2021.

92 "security breach": Scott Morrison, Press conference, Parliament House, Canberra, 23 March 2021.

92 Dutton and PMO briefed: "Don't Ask, Don't Tell", *Four Corners*, ABC TV, 22 March 2021.

92 Michaelia Cash: James Glenday, Andrew Probyn and Matthew Doran, "The big questions left unanswered about the alleged rape of Brittany Higgins at Parliament House", ABC (online), 21 February 2021.

93 nobody had ever told him: Scott Morrison, Doorstop interview, Parliament House, Canberra, 16 February 2021.

93 "In my experience": Myles Wearring, "Julie Bishop surprised neither Scott Morrison nor Christian Porter read anonymous letter detailing historical rape allegation denied by Porter", *7.30*, ABC TV, 8 March 2021.

93 "I find it incredible": Ally Foster, "Malcolm Turnbull says it's 'inconceivable' PM didn't know about rape allegations", News.com.au, 17 February 2021.

93 "as a father first": Scott Morrison, Doorstop interview, Parliament House, Canberra, 16 February 2021.

93 backgrounding: "Politics with Peter van Onselen", *RN Breakfast*, ABC Radio, 18 February 2021.

93 Kunkel review: Michelle Grattan, "View from the Hill: Morrison's top staffer doesn't find colleagues briefed against Higgins' partner but reminds them of 'standards'", *The Conversation*, 25 May 2021.

93 Kate Thornton's allegations: Louise Milligan, "Scott Morrison, senators and AFP told of historical rape allegation against Cabinet Minister", *Four Corners*, ABC TV, 26 February 2021.

94 "no matters": Scott Morrison, Press conference, Kirribilli, NSW, 1 March 2021.

94 "The detail", "happy to stand": "Minister under cloud of rape allegations to identify himself", *7.30*, ABC TV, 2 March 2021.

94 "Just imagine for a second": "Read the full press conference transcript, Christian Porter denies historical rape allegation", ABC (online), 3 March 2021.

95 "Terrible things": Scott Morrison, Press conference, Tomago, NSW, 4 March 2021.

95   "catapult us": Laura Tingle and James Elton, "Christian Porter's internal investigation into Dyson Heydon reveals more complaints", 7.30, ABC TV, 5 March 2021.

95   details of testimonies, "It happened to so many", "we talk about": Natassia Chrysanthos, "Hundreds of Sydney students claim they were sexually assaulted", *The Sydney Morning Herald*, 19 February 2021.

96   piece by David Hardaker: David Hardaker, "Here's one for an independent inquiry: did recovered memories target Christian Porter?", *Crikey*, 5 March 2021.

96   "exclusive", diary entries: Janet Albrechtsen and Peter van Onselen, "In her words: Kate's dossier of tragedy", *The Australian*, 12 March 2021.

97   "as credible as possible": Sharri Markson, Nicola Berkovic and Geoff Chambers, "Christian Porter to testify in rape 'trial' after launching defamation action against ABC and Louise Milligan", *The Australian*, 16 March 2021.

97   "take a hatchet", "takes pressure off", etc.: Benjamin Millar, Twitter, 15 March 2021, https://twitter.com/BenjaminMillar/status/1371249260281225218?s=20, accessed 1 November 2021.

97   DARVO: Nicola Heath, "What is 'DARVO' and how is it used against survivors of violence?", SBS (online), 5 May 2021.

97–98   "exquisitely screwed up": Leslie Canold, "How screwed up is our politics and media? A dead woman's treatment tells all", *Crikey*, 12 March 2021.

98   Brittany Higgins, March 4 Justice: "Read what Brittany Higgins had to say when she spoke at the women's march", ABC (online), 15 March 2021.

99   "met with bullets": "Scott Morrison speaks on March4Justice rallies, says protests elsewhere are 'met with bullets'", SBS (online), 15 March 2021.

99   "masturbating on the desk": Peter van Onselen, "Coalition staffer sacked over lewd sex acts after group 'filmed sex acts in Parliament House'", *The Australian*, 22 March 2021.

99   "enormity of the political trouble": "Laura Tingle on the Prime Minister's apology", 7.30, ABC TV, 23 March 2021.

100   Andrew Laming allegations: AAP, "Federal Liberal MP Andrew Laming apologises for online treatment of two Brisbane women", *Guardian Australia*, 26 March 2021.

100   "game changer": Scott Morrison, Press conference, Parliament House, Canberra, 8 April 2021.

100   "presiding over": Kristine Ziwica, "The Morrison government is quietly crab-walking back from its 'landmark' sexual harassment inquiry recommendations", *Women's Agenda*, 25 August 2021.

100   "failed to give funding": "Media release: Morrison Government fails to fund Working Women's Centres", Working Women's Agenda, 9 September 2021.

101   "The Good Society": Eden Gillespie, "Calls for 'confusing' sex ed site to be reviewed", *The Feed*, SBS TV, 21 April 2021.

101   "I'm no expert": Callum Goode, "'Clumsy' govt-backed consent video panned", *The Canberra Times*, 19 April 2021.

101   denied being consulted: Emma Brancatisano, "Government's consent videos featuring tacos and milkshakes slammed as 'concerning and confusing'", SBS (online), 19 April 2021.

101   "defamation trial of the century": Nicola Berkovic, "Christian Porter's defamation trial of the century", *The Australian*, 18 March 2021.

101   defamation trial settled: Michael McGowan, "Christian Porter agrees to discontinue defamation court case against ABC", *Guardian Australia*, 31 May 2021.

102   "my first mistake", "That I had", "Morrison rang me", etc.: "Liberal MP Julia Banks speaks on the toxic culture at Parliament House", 7.30, ABC TV, 5 July 2021.

102   "I'm supporting Julia": Scott Morrison, Doorstop interview, Sydney, 29 August 2018.

103   "It's hard to process": Grace Tame, "Porter's elevation betrays PM's chilling apathy towards survivors", *The Sydney Morning Herald*, 4 August 2021.

104   "Twitter mob": "Statement from Christian Porter", christianporter.com.au, 19 September 2021.

106   "fumbled": Katharine Murphy, "As gut-wrenching scandals shake the government, Scott Morrison fumbles when he should lead", *Guardian Australia*, 1 March 2021.

106   "Let me share", "patient women", etc.: Katharine Murphy, "Scott Morrison's efforts to engage with women are more 'me' than mea culpa", *Guardian Australia*, 27 March 2021.

106   Polling from Essential Media: 'Preferred Prime Minister', Essential report, 12 October 2021, https://essentialvision.com.au/tag/scott-morrison, accessed 5 November 2021.

107   "a marked", "hate-filled feminazi", etc.: Laura Bates, *Men Who Hate Women*, Simon & Schuster, London, 2020.

107   Incels – a group initially formed by men lamenting their lack of sexual and romantic options – are "involuntary celibates". The ideology is entirely untethered from its origins: men who identify as incels essentially believe that women should be punished for denying them their birthright to sex. Their online ravings have materialised into real-world killings: at last count, there had been at least eight mass murders by men identifying as incels. "Pick-up artists" form a $100-million global industry training men to trick and coerce women into having sex with them; its leaders have boasted about rape, and even advocate for

it to be legalised. "MGTOW" is a community who see women as "so toxic and dangerous" that men can only live freely if they have no contact with them.

109 "Most of the global warming posturing": Greg Callaghan, "Right-winger? Not me, says alt-right darling Jordan Peterson", *The Sydney Morning Herald*, 21 April 2018.

111 "Before our boys": "Why do they do it?", *The Trap* (podcast), Victorian Women's Trust, 11 August 2021.

112 "We essentially raise": Niobe Way, quoted in Elizabeth Blair, "Women are speaking up about harassment and abuse, but why now?", NPR, 27 October 2017.

113 "All patriarchal societies": "Government, Policy & Power", *The Trap* (podcast), Victorian Women's Trust, 15 September 2021.

116 "did something": Mike Willacy to Richard Fidler, in "Inside a rogue force", *Conversations*, ABC Radio, 18 August 2021.

116 "situates the toughest": Bruce Baer Arnold, "On a screen darkly: Outback noir, erasure and toxic masculinity", *Canberra Law Review*, vol. 16, no. 1, 2019.

117 untouchable music industry figures: Grace Tobin, Ali Russell and Lucy Carter, "Fired Sony Music executive Tony Glover speaks out over sexual harassment claims", *Four Corners*, ABC TV, 12 October 2021.

119 "secretive, proudly masculine culture", "shrouds law enforcement": Damien Cave and Isabella Kwai, "A sexual harasser spent years on Australia's top court, an inquiry finds", *The New York Times*, 23 June 2020.

120 "post-racial": Michael C. Dawson and Lawrence D. Bobo, "One year later and the myth of a postracial society", *Du Bois Review: Social Science Research on Race*, vol. 6, no. 2, pp. 247–49.

120 "fighting the patriarch": Susan Faludi, "The patriarchs are falling. The patriarchy is stronger than ever", *The New York Times*, 28 December 2017.

TOP BLOKES

Correspondence

Rachel Nolan

In *Top Blokes*, Lech Blaine applies his intellect and kind-hearted curiosity to an essential current of Australian identity, the myth of the larrikin: the anti-establishment figure (invariably male) who employs a "reckless collectivism," bringing mates together in the face of injustice.

Lech is from Toowoomba, but that's a conservative, uninteresting place. His worldview arises from the cultural identity of Ipswich, the working-class city his late parents came from and of which Lech's cousin Allan Langer remains the most celebrated son.

I'm from Ipswich, and as no one's written about the city since the now ageing poet Thomas Shapcott, Lech's interest in the place makes my heart sing. The story of Ipswich is the story of class, identity and labourism in Australia.

The Labor Party was born in Barcaldine in 1891, but before that, in 1888, Australia's first Labor MP emerged from Ipswich when Thomas Glassey, a coalmining unionist describing himself as "independent Labor," won the seat of Bundamba in the Queensland parliament.

In 1899, the region contributed members to the world's first Labor government, that of Queensland premier Anderson Dawson.

From 1915 to 1948, the workers of Ipswich were represented by Frank Cooper, an eight-hour-day campaigner who became treasurer in the reforming government of William Forgan Smith. Elected in 1932, that government rejected the austerity of the Premiers' Plan, rebuilt Queensland in Art Deco style and entrenched the state as the highest wage, highest-taxing jurisdiction in the country. As premier himself in 1942, Cooper stood by Labor prime minister John Curtin through World War II.

Ipswich produced Queensland's first Labor woman MP when Vi Jordan was elected member for Ipswich West in 1966. She was backed by mining and rail unions, all-male workforces. Years after her death, Vi Jordan's son told me about the atmosphere of the times, how Gough Whitlam would stay with the family when visiting the city as federal Opposition leader, and how the house would be filled with excited and erudite conversation as unionists, directly influenced by the more radical British socialist movement, envisaged a program of industrial relations reform, free public health and free tertiary education.

In 1977, Bill Hayden, a working-class policeman from Ipswich, became leader of the federal parliamentary Labor Party. Hayden had already built the structure of Medicare as health minister before seeking to salvage economic policy as Whitlam's last treasurer. As Opposition leader, Bill Hayden built the foundations of the modern Labor Party, socially progressive but economically robust. He was replaced by Bob Hawke on the day writs were issued for the 1983 poll, with Hawke winning the election Hayden himself said "a drover's dog" could have won.

The Hawke and Keating years coincided with, but didn't cause, Ipswich's deindustrialisation. From the 1970s, coalmining moved to the Bowen Basin, and electric trains didn't require local workshops employing 3000 men. Ipswich people resented economic liberalisation and were suss on Paul Keating's Zegna suits. The politics of class shifted from economic to cultural identity.

After Hayden's preferred successor, a working-class boy and Rhodes scholar named David Hamill, missed out on federal preselection in a shonky factional stitch-up, the ALP lost the Ipswich-based seat of Oxley to Pauline Hanson in 1996.

She remains our gift to the nation.

By the 2000s, unionism in Ipswich had collapsed. The Labour Day march was a shadow of its former self, and the Trades Hall, the original building with its wrought-iron verandahs having been replaced by a jerry-built concrete block in the 1980s, gradually became empty.

With the city becoming a commuter satellite of Brisbane and its working-class identity adrift, the political void was filled by populism. The new mayor, Paul Pisasale, developed a classic larrikin persona, taking the longstanding resentment of class and directing it towards an "other" defined by geography rather than income. Pisasale's schtick was that Ipswich people should be proud of where they came from, sticking it to sneering outsiders, including those from Brisbane. He was making Ipswich great again.

As a member of the ALP, Pisasale neutralised Ipswich's only potential source of organised political opposition, but did little for the city or working people. As his cult of personality grew, Pisasale was re-elected with as much as 87 per cent of the vote, making him the most popular politician in Australia. Under his mayoralty, property development became Ipswich's boom industry, the city sprawled and the CBD became derelict. He's now serving seven years for official corruption related to taking cash from developers and for sexual assault.

While Pisasale's populist cult is an extreme example, the truth is that every one of Australia's large former industrial cities has seen some kind of scandal combining elements of populism, sex, property developers and/or larrikins.

In Wollongong, a sex-for-development-approval scandal contributed to the downfall of the last state Labor government. The Newcastle mayor, a property developer, resigned after he was caught funnelling secret donations to Liberal MPs, and Geelong Council has just emerged from administration after the council, dominated by a former paparazzo turned larrikin, was sacked for bullying and failing to provide good government.

Once, the local politics of these places would have been defined by class, with an active civic culture characterised by unions and Labor activists on one side and chambers of commerce and service clubs on the other. Lech is right to say Australia's working-class towns have held together better than Trump's Pennsylvania or the Brexit-voting north of England, but it's a near-run thing. There is, as the councils have shown, a constant vulnerability to shysters.

Lech Blaine's thesis is a simple one: that Anthony Albanese, with his working-class authenticity, may neutralise the culture wars through which conservatives separate educated Labor representatives from their working-class base. Perhaps, he says, by staying mum on coal and Instagramming photos of tinned peas and corn on his plate, the dinky-di Albo can defeat ScoMo, an entirely confected character whose feigned interest in rugby league disguises a puritanical rah-rah from the Eastern Suburbs.

I hope, of course, that Lech is right. Surely Labor can defeat a government that has systematically suppressed wages while delivering tax cuts that most benefit the rich, that has endangered our economy and security by stirring up China while dropping the ball on critical relationships in Southeast Asia, and that caused half the country to be needlessly locked down for months through its incompetent management of the vaccine rollout?

Not having a crystal ball, I don't know if it can. What I do know, having spent a good part of my working life representing Ipswich, is that the cultural markers as they're currently defined are hard to cut through. I was never so shameless as to feign passionate interest in rugby league, but my earnest commitment to social justice and good economic policy was no competition for the vacuous identity politics of the uber-larrikin Pisasale. A solid voting record on IR reform, public education and public health is harder to sell when there's no sense that class is an economic phenomenon and justice can only be achieved through collective action. The term I decided I didn't want to run again was the term I bought an Alfa.

It must be possible for Australia to get beyond the mindless and divisive identity wars that lure working Australians to vote against their own economic interests and for a smaller, meaner country. We can do so either by seeking, as Albanese has, to neutralise the most shallow of cultural markers or by elevating the elements of cultural identity that unite us in an expansive vision: the Olympic team, an affinity with the landscape, the music of Paul Kelly.

That musician is, in my view, the great storyteller and unifier of Australian popular culture. In 1998, as John Howard was turning his back on Aboriginal reconciliation, Kelly wrote "Little Kings," a song about how power is exercised, how lies told as history can alter our sense of identity and about how, everywhere, warning bells ring out across the lucky country:

> In the land of the little kings, justice doesn't mean a thing and everywhere the little kings are getting away with murder.

Rachel Nolan

TOP BLOKES

Correspondence

Bri Lee

Lately I've been thinking a lot about universities in Australia, the various roles they play and why they are so loved by some and loathed by others. In my latest book, I refer to this as the "chimera of the campus." Some see a hotbed of Marxist hippies in the making, others see a funnelling of wealth and power to the same narrow elite political class. Somewhere between the two are the champagne socialists, latte-sipping lefties, the stealth conservatives and the bulk of the upwardly mobile middle class. The current federal Liberal Party appears to be doing what it can to eviscerate the tertiary sector, yet the Young Liberals in most states meet and recruit in those very quads under those very sandstone towers.

Lech's brother, John, tells Lech how people talk down to him when they find out that he and his friends don't have uni degrees and that he sends his kids to the local public school. "'Labor became a party for people who went to uni,' says John, 'As people get more educated, they get more opinionated. But even if what you're saying is factually true, it doesn't mean that I need to agree with you.'" Lech surmises that the contempt John "feels emanating from progressives isn't an anecdotal anomaly." And, thanks to the wonders of compulsory voting, "every three years, John gets the chance to prove that his opinion has equal weight to those of our university-educated brother and sister who vote for the Greens."

The rich and complex legacy of Enlightenment ideals flows through universities and presents itself as the baseline ideology from which anything else is an aberration. When a "highly educated" person hears someone such as John reject factual evidence in favour of his own opinion, they immediately translate this as a kind of fundamental idiocy. Anyone who denies climate change is a moron, and only the thick-skulled opposed marriage equality, and if you believe a woman's place is mothering and home-keeping you are simply an idiot. When the highly educated disagree with someone, their automatic response is to discredit their opponent, often in language that attempts to suggest they are less intelligent somehow. The "bogan" judgement is a part of this, as a lower level or "quality" of education has become tellingly synonymous with those outside of major cities and with less money. In doing all this, the highly educated person's own value system is invisible to them and hyper-visible to those they are speaking down to. John could afford to send his daughters to a fancy private school but doesn't, because he would rather they grow up knowing that "hard work and being a good person" are what make you successful in life. Lech is right in writing that "contempt" towards people such as John "emanates" from progressives. We progressives like to think that our derision is only ever reactionary – that the "bogans" do the "bad things" first, and then we try to teach them how to think and do things the "right way." But the uncomfortable question that John's story raises is just how much us insufferably opinionated progressives are driving the rest of the country further to the right.

In the aftermath of the last federal election, I moved from Queensland to New South Wales and felt a pretty big difference in the response and attitudes on the ground. In Brisbane, I had the sense that the metropolitan lefties were the minority of the state. In Sydney, everyone was incredulous and outraged that a small bunch of rednecks up north had somehow managed to ruin everything for everyone else. I was invited onto ABC's *The Drum* to discuss the result, and tried (in vain) to explain in a soundbite what Lech Blaine achieves spectacularly in *Top Blokes*: progressives can be so excruciatingly condescending. Everyone was acting shocked by the results coming out of Queensland, but it had been a long time since anyone actually asked Queenslanders what they wanted and stuck around to listen to the answers. Queensland is a string of large satellite cities, each with its own identity and needs. It's rare to see anyone from Cairns, Townsville, Bundaberg or Rockhampton on the ABC, and certainly not on *The Drum*, where everyone sat, apparently confounded that they didn't know their compatriots. Young progressives took to social media, exploding with outrage and disappointment and exhaustion, cursing the "bogans."

The split Lech documents among his own siblings is, I believe, extraordinarily representative of a large cross-section of Australians. Many of us experience a version of it when we go home for Christmas with our own families. There are ABC articles with titles such as "How to Deal with a Racist Uncle at Christmas," and when I see them being shared online I have the impression they are being read by people with degrees in preparation for difficult conversations with those without them. This makes for an often impossible balance of goals and ideals: people of colour have no obligation to debate with racists and no duty to try to "convince" someone they are their equal. Similarly, it is not fair that women asking for equality in the home and workplace need to tread on eggshells around the hurt feelings of the conservatives, and in no way would I ever suggest that the LGBTQIA+ community aren't "doing enough" to bridge the gap between their future and the people who like the prejudiced past. But Lech's essay gave me the immense satisfaction of having articulated something I'd been fumbling around and towards for a long time: just because people on the left have ideas that move us towards a better collective future does not mean our superiority complex is justified or useful. If we don't pull our heads in and find better methods, we drive away the people we must bring with us. White progressives must talk to other white people about racial equality, the straights need to take more of the load on issues of gender and sexuality, and men must step the fuck up and talk to other men about women.

I believe that we need to treat global warming as the emergency it is. I believe children under the age of five have the right to free and universal care and education. I believe we could and should take ten times the number of refugees that we currently do, and that we'd be better for it. Death to kings and tax the rich. All of it. But if we, the progressive left, continue to belittle people who think differently, we will remain doomed, perpetually in opposition in both government and life.

Having spent the last three years researching the role the education system plays in our ideas of intelligence and worth, I see where the left–right split often calcifies: between those who attended university and those who didn't. One of the best things about the Enlightenment was the wrangling of power away from the church. A failing of the Enlightenment's contemporary followers is their presumption that their own capacity for "reason" is inherently superior. The data prove the almighty correlation between level of educational attainment and voting behaviour. What the left often don't want to acknowledge is how we use this as shorthand evidence for the stupidity and wholesale inferiority of the right.

Bri Lee

TOP BLOKES

Correspondence

David Hunt

Scott Morrison is a dingo in sheep's clothing. Lech Blaine's Quarterly Essay leaves us in no doubt that the chickens of the PM's self-publicised coop should be wary whenever their jailer ambles towards them with a carefully curated bowl of kitchen scraps – and not just on curry night.

On this subject, *Top Blokes: The Larrikin Myth, Class and Power* presents nothing new. Politicians pretend their way to power? Who'd have thunk it? While Morrison's masquerading as "a typical Aussie bloke" who loves a beer at the Sharkies' game is disingenuous – and coming up with his own nickname (after road-testing it with a focus group of men in shiny vests) is just plain sad – these deceptions pale in comparison to those of some of Australia's early Labor leaders.

In 1886, Chris Watson left New Zealand for Sydney, where he found work mucking out Government House's stables. Seventeen years later, with an intuitive understanding of the connection between government and shovelling shit, he became prime minister of Australia and the world's first Labor/Labour national leader. Watson didn't just give himself a new nickname – he manufactured a whole new identity. No one knew that Kiwi Chris Watson was really Chilean John Tanck until after his death. Tanck, who had a non-British father and had never applied for British citizenship, would have known he was constitutionally ineligible to sit in the Australian parliament, let alone serve as prime minister.

King O'Malley, Labor's minister for home affairs in the 1910 Fisher government, was another proto-Barnaby. This is, of course, a reference to O'Malley's foreign citizenship excluding him from the Australian parliament and is in no way intended to imply that Barnaby had home affairs (he appears to have used his workplace and discreet motels). O'Malley, the man responsible for constructing the national capital in a frozen sheep paddock, pretended to be a respectable British Canadian, rather than an insurance salesman from Kansas.

Thomas Walker was a Labor man who actually did come to Australia from Canada ... to escape a manslaughter charge. A coronial inquiry found the young medium had killed a combustible seance attendee who'd come into contact with the phosphorous he used to make "spiritual lights." In 1877, Walker fled to Melbourne, where he delivered the first of a series of Australian spiritualist lectures, during which he claimed to be possessed by the spirit of Giordano Bruno, a Dominican friar, cosmologist and occultist burned at the stake in 1600 for saying sacramental wine was not the blood of Christ and Mary was not a virgin. In 1892, while a NSW member of parliament, he was charged with shooting and wounding a clergyman while drunk. None of this stopped Thomas Walker serving as a West Australian Labor attorney-general and minister for justice and education.

Politicians who lied about their name or nationality, or claimed to be an undead Italian heretic, make Morrison's frauds on the Australian public seem milder than one of his chicken curries. But the falsehoods of these early MPs were essentially personal in nature and didn't interfere with their policy platforms.

Some other early Australian leaders abandoned ideology and jettisoned principle for political gain. Joseph Cook, the first leader of the NSW parliamentary Labor Party, ditched the silent "e" in his name as an ostentation unbefitting a working man. He then ditched being a working man, joining, and later leading, the Free Trade Party; becoming prime minister as leader of the anti-Labor and anti–free trade Liberal Party; and again turning coat to serve as deputy prime minister in the Nationalist government of Billy Hughes.

Hughes, another Labor man turned political weathervane, represented six parties during his parliamentary career, leading five of them. Prime Minister Robert Menzies once commented that Hughes had been a member of every political party, at which point Arthur Fadden interjected he'd never joined his Country Party. Hughes, showing that what he lacked in political consistency he made up for with a sense of humour, retorted, "I had to draw the line somewhere, didn't I?"

I reference these Labor men (and they were all men for a long while) not to attack their party or ideology, or to pump the wheels of the Coalition bus, but to make the point that Morrison is merely at the tail of a conga line of suckholes of all political stripes.

Politicians should not be criticised for changing their views over time or in response to altered circumstances, but Cook and Hughes arguably ditched their core political beliefs for personal political gain. In fairness to Morrison, he can't be accused of ditching his core political beliefs, because he's never held any. No Australian politician, even one-armed Peter Lalor, has had Morrison's facility for not holding things. His capacity to say one thing and then declare the opposite, while unashamedly maintaining his position has never changed, is unrivalled in Australian political history. While another conservative leader was not for turning, Morrison is not for sticking. He is human Teflon.

Many Australians recognise this. The question is: why do they put up with it? Lech Blaine is right in laying the blame, at least in part, on "the identity crisis at the heart of Australia," although he over-eggs the larrikin pudding.

One of the issues I have with Blaine's eminently readable and enjoyable essay is that while he accuses Morrison, Hawke and other powerful people of hijacking the larrikin for personal gain, Blaine also appropriates the larrikin. He projects aspects of the current larrikin image (egalitarianism and disregard for convention) back in time and suggests larrikins shared a strong affinity with the working class and labour movement. A reader of Blaine's essay would be left with the impression that striking shearers, bush poets such as Banjo Paterson and Henry Lawson, bushranger Ned Kelly, writer Miles (aka Stella) Franklin and feminist Vida Goldstein were all larrikins.

The term "larrikin" first appeared in print in Melbourne in 1870. Larrikins were not knockabout blokes who called a spade a spade – they were disaffected young people who formed loose gangs, known as "forties" and then "pushes". The larrikin was a "yob" – that is, a boy in the back slang of the English costermongers (mobile grocers with attitude) whom the larrikins modelled themselves on. "Yob" came to mean a lout or hooligan, because that is what larrikins were. Following the 1886 sexual assault of Mary Jane Hicks by members of the Waterloo Push, and a series of similar offences, they were popularly perceived as gang rapists.

While most nineteenth-century larrikins had "working-class" backgrounds, they were generally unskilled labourers – tuppenny capitalists who disdained those who'd learnt a trade. They loathed the labour movement, and the emerging trade unions loathed them in return. Larrikins disrupted union parades and pickets, hurling abuse and rotten food at the marching or striking workers. Causing mayhem at union picnics was a favourite larrikin sport.

The nihilism at the heart of larrikin culture drew them to the legend of Ned Kelly, a man whose charisma and showmanship elevated him from being a poor, horse-thieving, police-murdering terrorist with a penchant for cast-iron fetish wear into Australia's answer to Robin Hood. The "larrikin class was strongly represented" at the 5 November 1880 Melbourne rally that called for the government to commute the bushranger's death sentence, but Kelly was in no way a larrikin. He was country, while the larrikins were very much city.

Bushmen were not larrikins. The striking shearers did not see larrikins as co-revolutionaries in the war between labour and capital but as self-indulgent, antisocial townies. Banjo Paterson painted larrikins as vicious urban thugs in "Uncle Bill: The Larrikin's Lament", with Henry Lawson doing likewise in "The Captain of the Push." Larrikins, like many other Australians, were drawn to the professional sports that emerged in the late nineteenth and early twentieth centuries, in particular boxing and Australian Rules football, and later rugby league. Lawson saw the Australian obsession with sport over the arts as a blight, writing in "A Song of Southern Writers":

> In the land where sport is sacred, where the lab'rer is a god,
> You must pander to the people, make a hero of a clod!

Lawson was in no way a larrikin. Neither was his protégé and fellow writer Miles Franklin. Franklin was a deep thinker and keen social observer, while larrikins cultivated an air of insular anti-intellectualism. Vida Goldstein, like Franklin, was a feminist – a charge that could never be levelled at larrikins, who the popular press accused of demeaning and assaulting their "donahs" or "tarts", as women who inhabited the edges of larrikin society were known. Goldstein was unabashedly intellectual and passionate about politics and improving Australian society, again areas into which larrikins rarely strayed.

Nobody liked a larrikin, not even other larrikins, with the most vicious larrikin assaults reserved for members of rival pushes. Strangely, it was the arts, not sport, that began the rehabilitation of the larrikin image, first with music-hall larrikin acts in the late nineteenth century, then with the writing of C.J. Dennis, whose Sentimental Bloke and Ginger Mick were uncomplicated working-class blokes with hearts, dreams and aspirations. World War I gave rise to the larrikin digger trope, an irreverent bloke whose dishevelled dress showed his disrespect for the British officers he served under. As larrikins stopped their street brawls and shooting each other in the late 1920s, the larrikin menace faded, and the larrikin mantle settled on the shoulders of the knockabout anti-authoritarian male.

Blaine's historical larrikin is myth, as is his story of the foundation of the Australian Labor Party, a fable nurtured by generations of Labor men and women, most of whom undoubtedly believe it to be true. Blaine traces the ALP back to the 1891 striking shearers who gathered in the Queensland town of Barcaldine – and the shearers' 1891 May Day march and reading of the Manifesto of the Queensland Labour Party to a gathering of workers under the Barcaldine ghost gum on 9 September 1892 – undoubtedly key moments in the history of the Australian labour movement.

However, this myth ignores the NSW origin story, which traces the birth of the party to quarryman Charles Hart convening the first Labour Electoral League meeting at Balmain's Unity Hall Hotel on 4 April 1891. South Australians, by contrast, insist they founded the Labor Party, when the United Trades and Labor Council met on 7 January 1891 (almost certainly at a far creepier location than a pub or a tree) to form the United Labor Party of South Australia. All and none of these foundation stories are true. There was no angelic trumpet, or even the drunken cry of a striking shearer tripping over an unshorn sheep, to herald Labor's birth. There were instead a number of meetings of unionists, socialists and radicals, held across the colonies, where it was agreed that industrial action, in the absence of political representation, was no longer sufficient to advance workers' rights.

The fact is the Queensland origin story is more romantic – and it has a tree in it, a key element in many origin myths. Labor even named the ghost gum "The Tree of Knowledge," a blatant biblical rip-off. The Queensland story was a deliberate attempt by Labor's founding fathers to link the party to the biggest Australian myth of all – the bush legend – a myth so powerful that it made citizens of the most urbanised society on earth (if you ignored First Nations people) build a common identity around the idealised bushman, his stoic wife and their golden-haired, ruddy-cheeked children, a myth with the power to make a mild-mannered Sydney accountant who owned an Akubra think he was the Man from Snowy River.

The emerging labour movement latched onto the bush legend like a blowfly to a jumbuck's jacksy, hoping that a little of its magic would rub off. As acknowledged by William Guthrie Spence, foundation president of the Amalgamated Shearers' Union of Australasia and a founding father of Labor:

> Labor ... is a political as well as a propagandist movement. Its leaders realise that before we can have social reform the people must be educated to demand and carry out ... reforms ... It is slow work getting the right ideas knocked into the masses. They are mostly so mentally lazy that they take their views ready-made from a misleading press.

Blaine's essay identifies a number of other key Australian myths, in particular that Australians are naturally anti-authoritarian, a myth closely tied to that of the larrikin. Australians, as acknowledged by Blaine, are one of the most law-abiding people on earth. From the foundation of the convict colony of New South Wales, government provided services that were delivered by churches, charities, friendly societies or private enterprise in other societies. Despite these services, and the administrations and budgets that grew to provide them, the residents of the

Australian colonies paid no direct taxes until Victoria introduced a modest land tax in 1877. The Australian colonies led the world in establishing the modern secret ballot, postal voting, full women's suffrage, independent electoral bodies and a host of other reforms that increased public confidence in government and its institutions. Most Australians have accordingly been historically trusting of the state, its institutions and, sometimes regrettably, its politicians.

Australians' willingness to embrace myths have allowed them to reinvent themselves. Their desire to rinse the convict stain from the moral fabric of the nation, which remained strong until the late 1970s, led them to fabricate their own family histories, replacing ancestral handkerchief thieves with sturdy farmers, adventurers and down-on-their luck aristocrats. They pushed the inconvenient truths of the dispossession and frontier murder of First Nations people, and of White Australia, to the back of their collective consciousness and conscience, embracing John Howard's 1996 "Bex, a cuppa and a good lie down" mantra that we should feel "comfortable and relaxed about our past, as the balance sheet of our history is one of heroic achievement."

Blaine cites Clare Wright, one of Australia's most compelling and insightful historians, as arguing that Labor can't "consistently win federal government until it tells a coherent story that links back to deeper myths about Australian identity." I respectfully disagree. My view is that we Australians and the politicians that serve us should not attach ourselves to myths, but to truth.

Our susceptibility to myth-making allows us to accept the bush and larrikin legends, and their appropriation by elites. It allows us to embrace the myth of anti-authoritarianism, without asking difficult questions of those in authority. It allows us to look inwards on our own self-created realities, as we lock out the world from Fortress Australia, lock out the "new foreigners" of the other Australian states from our resurrected parochial fiefdoms and lock out the disadvantaged and the dispossessed from our McMansions.

Blaine cites Russel Ward's 1958 *The Australian Legend*, which concluded that the "typical Australian" "believes that Jack is not only as good as his master but, at least in principle, probably a good deal better." Sixty-three years later, it's now, "I'm alright, Jack."

Until we Australians look beyond our own self-interest, discard myths for truths and accept our past in all its beauty and its terror, we will be condemned to a stunted present and an even more diminished future. We will turn a deaf ear to the lies of politicians such as Morrison as long as they comfort us with platitudes about being at the front of the queue and being the best people in the world. We get the politicians we deserve.

David Hunt

TOP BLOKES

Correspondence

Alison Pennington

Lech Blaine tells a convincing story about how big business and conservative politicians co-opt and thieve working-class culture. But that culture first had to be built and *exist* in order to be stolen. Who made it? The substance of "larrikinism" is never really defined. It is apparently simultaneously anti-establishment, egalitarian, republican, collectivist, racist, hypermasculine and drunk. Now, my brain, hardwired for materialism, says cultural traditions are most powerfully understood as the fruits of people's economic foundations. It means that the way people think, talk and understand themselves is shaped by their access to what they need for a secure, good life: jobs, incomes, housing, essential services.

Egalitarianism, the fair go and "taking the piss" didn't emerge spontaneously. These cultural forms relied on redistributive collectivist institutions such as centralised wage-setting and unionism – countervailing powers to employers and powerful coercive government. These institutions were built through enormous struggles against convict transportation, the nineteenth-century *Master and Servant Acts* and 120 years of punitive laws funnelling cheap labour to lazy businessmen for easy profits. By confronting the hostile, disciplinary colonial state, workers over time received a fair wage for the value they created on the job – a fairer share of the pie. The coverage of egalitarian legislation such as the awards was patchy and often excluded Aboriginal people, women and migrant workers. Social movements, particularly from the late 1960s, started setting that right, achieving welfare-state expansion on the way. Aboriginal people had, of course, resisted colonial administration for much longer. We can find the basis for "Australianisms" here.

Larrikinism is a cultural artefact of a population that won sufficient jobs, income to buy beer, time to drink it and a welfare safety net. It's distinctly working-class. We got here because life in Australia made collectivism critical to survival, and collectivism makes vibrant culture. By working, joining unions, participating in community groups, sports and churches, working people create shared language, flair, humour and a strong sense of self.

Convict roots

This year, Cricket Australia announced it would drop the promotion of "Australia Day" from its upcoming Big Bash League. Prime Minister Scott Morrison responded by recasting his ancestral convict roots to discredit Aboriginal justice. It was shocking new terrain for conservatives in modern Australian colonial politics. Convict history is traditionally the terrain of collective politics.

Tony Moore's *Death or Liberty* documents the history of political prisoners sent as convicts to Australia. It's an authoritative account that supports Australia's title as one of the oldest democracies in the world. By the eighteenth century, British prisons were bursting at the seams with political dissidents, peasants and workers resisting enclosures and occupation, and advocating for workers' suffrage and unionism. Thousands were locked up for crimes of theft, treason, riot, incitement, seditious libel and more. Many crimes were punishable by death. But with mass democratic movements and political independence in full swing, the British preferred transportation to creating martyrs. So they sent them to Australia. Convict resistance imbued the labour movement with the ideals of radical democracy and republicanism. These political programs would in turn foster Australian egalitarian, anti-establishment values. Australian democracy was only ever partial until Aboriginal peoples obtained basic civil rights, and the pursuit of justice and self-determination continues.

Real Australian history has been erased time and again. Scott Morrison tried to reconstitute Australia as classic American entrepreneurial republicanism: convicts were actually free settlers of the New World "having a go, getting a go." But of course, Australia was established as a giant prison for the British Empire on stolen land. A dark organ of discipline. We may no longer hold dominion status, but the government's penchant for violent imprisonment remains today. Aboriginal people are incarcerated at a higher rate than black South Africans were during apartheid. We lock up children as young as ten in juvenile prisons, most of them Aboriginal and a majority yet to be convicted of any crime; refugees are locked up in private offshore prisons. Serco is like a modern-day East India Company.

The purpose of uncovering our submerged history isn't to stoke oppression complexes but to best understand who we are (and aren't). As workers increasingly defect to right-wing populism (as we've seen in the United States, Europe, the United Kingdom and now parts of Australia), celebrating world-leading traditions of resistance, against all odds, can support the rebuilding of something broader and better.

Women make history

Top Blokes tells a story of larrikinism made by men and dismantled by men. It's in the title, after all. But who makes our working-class history? Women have made tremendous contributions to Australia's egalitarian cultural traditions – in unions, social movements and civil society organisations. If we don't acknowledge that our collectivist history was made by all people – men, women, First Nations people and migrants – we miss a great deal. Historian Clare Wright's work is scattered throughout Blaine's essay, though her call to (re)interpret history with attention to the agency of women and other marginalised groups isn't observed. For instance, Blaine says that since Victoria has "no convict stain," the prevalence of larrikinism there is due to "testosterone more than political ideology." Wright's work, along with that of many other writers and activists, shows that when it comes to forging proud collectivist traditions of mateship, solidarity, sacrifice and service, women played leading roles. They were never bystanders. In *Beyond the Ladies Lounge*, Wright documents women's dominance and visibility in Australian hotel-keeping, especially in Victoria; pubs are playgrounds for larrikinism.

Far from a purely masculine display of bravado, larrikinism and egalitarian culture exist in Victoria because the trade union movement has historically been strongest there. It still is. A related and regrettable omission from Blaine's essay is women's leading role in union revitalisation. Surely the top candidate for Australia's bona fide flag-bearer of anti-establishment larrikinism is the ACTU's secretary, Sally McManus – a straight talker with a mullet, who in her first national media interview said bad laws should be broken. It shocked small-l liberal respectability and sent the political class, business lobbyists and technocrats into meltdown. It was a hat tip to the larrikin. It is important to note that the average union member today is a middle-aged woman working in health care. If unions were obstructed by the Accords and enterprise bargaining (by plenty of Top Blokes in leadership), then independent unionism is now being painstakingly remade by women in increasingly feminised services sectors.

Allow me to peer behind another gendered depiction of history, this time on personal terrain. My middle name is Kelly. I was raised with music and poems about one of Australia's most potent, captivating characters. The working class in Adelaide's west I grew up with embraced Ned's tragic and inspiring story. But it wasn't just Ned. It was all the Kellys. And the Kellys were a matriarchal family – headed by Ellen. Kate, Ned's little sister, rode as decoy for the Kelly Gang and campaigned with thousands to spare Ned's life. Ned advocated for the economically deprived underclass, the downtrodden of north-eastern Victoria – many

Irish-Catholics of convict stock – but it was the impossibility of delivering economic security for his mum and siblings that led him to collective conclusions. The centrality of familial women in Ned's egalitarian convictions is a big reason Peter Carey was criticised for fabricating a love interest in the literary masterpiece *The True History of the Kelly Gang*. In short, Neddy isn't everything.

Who dismantled it?

Having toured some of the historical terrain that made egalitarianism, we might now ask who dismantled it. Working people take pride in the hard work of creating culture and distinctly Australian cultural forms (rather than merely transplanting high art from overseas). Entry to this exciting world doesn't depend on your capacity to buy into it. In contrast, higher income classes don't need collectivism to survive. Culture for the rich is more akin to consumption choices. Accordingly, John Howard and Scott Morrison are of an ilk that doesn't generate culture but *consumes* it. And it's exactly what they've done. Howard most powerfully reconstituted working-class identity. Mateship was no longer about unionism, but something diggers did while fighting imperial wars for our freedoms. "Battlers" worked hard, head down, and accepted stagnant wages, insecure work and longer working hours as their lot in life. House prices doubled, and that's gotta be good, right? It's startling, really: what began as an independent, republican national pulse was coopted by ardent monarchists.

But cultural dissolution started long before Howard. Blaine's attention to the Hawke–Keating years is his strongest work. What allowed Bob Hawke to pursue his larger-than-life larrikin persona? Over 50 per cent unionisation. That's a mighty force of validation, and an organ to communicate your politics. Unions – the "industrial wing" of the ALP – were a ballast against rising individualisation in political leadership, observed increasingly in places such as the United States. But the unions were severely damaged by the Accords. In many respects, Hawke struck one of the most effective and powerful blows to egalitarian culture. The whip-smart, beer-sculling Rhodes scholar gave workers a false sense of security. The welfare state was retrenched, financial powers deregulated and the capacity of unions to hold Hawke accountable curtailed. Union militancy was partly cashed out for some decent reforms, such as Medicare and superannuation. But they didn't compensate for what was lost in wage-setting power. Hawke's incomes policies reduced the capacity of unions, which helped workers think and act for themselves. Consequently, workers became less discerning and more defenceless – university-educated professionals working sixty-hour weeks included. Our 1980s hangover is long-lasting.

As Blaine documents, individualist frames, rather than parties and policies, became the substance of our politics, as seen very clearly in the 2019 election. Bill Shorten was dripping with pro-worker policies, but the breakdown of the union infrastructure needed to communicate them and foster trust in the parliamentary process left him wide open to personality smear campaigns. Morrison's infrastructure? He's got the Pentecostal Church, business lobby groups and the Murdoch media to boot.

Hawke appealed to the fruits of working-class power (leisure time, mateship) while setting in motion forces that led to their eventual dismantling. In that sense, Hawke's economic policies paved the way for Morrison. Mass cultural forms stopped evolving. Instead, working-class Australian culture became stagnant – especially white working-class culture, which was forged around plentiful work, rising wages and solidarity. That cultural rump was left festering and vulnerable to manipulation by those with real economic power. The "radical larrikin" was extinguished by the "aesthetic larrikin." And that started long before #ScottyFromMarketing.

What are we salvaging?

Mass economic disempowerment has certainly degraded Australian cultural forms. Of course, our culture is full of less desirable facets, Australians' penchant for excessive drinking being one. (Though for this we can largely thank forty-odd decades of "wartime morality" achieved by prohibitionists, which forced pubs to close at 6 p.m., entrenching heavy-drinking sessions among workers from 5 to 6 p.m.) Beyond drinking, Blaine's depiction of working-class culture cannot be called universal. Gambling certainly isn't uniform. Nor sports. I had to write down the difference between rugby league (working-class) and union (upper-class), and refer back to my notes at least twice while reading the essay. In our other glorious national sport (Australian Rules), players from private and public schools, city and country, battle on the same field, although even that inclusiveness is narrowing. Anti-intellectualism isn't universal either. Nor is New South Wales' fondness for darkened windows in pubs (is the intention to elicit shame in patrons for all the pokies inside?). Pubs in southern states? Glorious, homely temples.

See what I'm getting at here? Where you live in Australia matters. And working-class culture isn't homogenous. Blaine's account of workers' decline rests on distinctly eastern-state economic and political trends. It mirrors the terrain of Australian federal politics, which has become increasingly centred on New South Wales and Queensland. But states have diverged considerably in recent decades.

For instance, Blaine accounts for rising right-wing political conservatism in regional New South Wales and Queensland by pointing to deindustrialisation. But that doesn't explain why manufacturing job losses in southern states didn't create a reactionary political base.

But what underpins celebratory drinking is working people's success in winning *leisure time* to drink. Victories include the eight-hour day, paid holiday leave and penalty rates for unsociable hours of work. If Australians haven't discovered yet who we are or what we're about, beyond time to booze, then we clearly need more time, income and resources to do that. But we're hamstrung. Since the 1980s, bipartisan policies have reduced wage growth, stifled economic democracy, increased inequality and killed "good jobs." In fact, research from the Centre for Future Work shows that those with a good job – that is, full-time work, with standard holiday and sick-pay entitlements – are now the minority of Australians. The mechanisms for elevating workers' voices, from the ground up to the suits, have been weakened.

Rather than throwing the baby out with the bathwater, as Clare Wright reminds us, we should identify the elements we want to salvage and build upon in creating a new future of collectivist politics. Revitalising culture means expanding economic security for all: plenty of good, meaningful jobs (including for artists), decent pay and strong public investment in income support and other necessities of life, such as housing, health care and education. Thankfully, underlying support for the social contract of good work and fair taxation is still strong in Australia. The 2021 Australia Talks survey shows 88 per cent of Australians believe job security is a problem for the country, and 63 per cent think the minimum wage should be higher. Research by the Australia Institute shows the majority want to fund more social services by collecting more tax, especially from big business and higher-income earners. If one thing is clear as day in Blaine's essay, it is this: progressives can't win on culture, and ought to get firmly back on economic terrain.

Bridging divides

Many have been bedazzled by Morrison's "everyman" performance. It's viewed as political mastery because decades of neoliberal economic policies have increased inequality and stratified society. We can't see each other fully anymore. We work different jobs (if working at all). Our runaway housing market geographically separates people by income. If those empowered with the resources and education to speak could actually see the bottom half of Australia, they'd have known Morrison was a shallow charade from day one. Instead, the precarious working poor, the low-paid welfare class, are viewed as policy problems, not as people with agency and an acute awareness that successive governments are failing them. It's worth recalling that the 1930s Depression only meant crushing poverty and destitution for people at the bottom. Most middle- and higher-income Australians continued their lives relatively unscathed.

To respond to our immediate challenges, save ourselves and our environment, and heal historical wounds, Australians must be able to answer the questions "Who are we?" and "What can we be proud of?" Australian values belong to the anti-establishment, ground-up democracy of everyday people. It is the only way we have ever made progress and the only path forward today.

Blaine's essay is one of the most engaging analyses I've read of Australian contemporary class relations. As a working-class woman straddling worlds, "suffocating from class consciousness," still filtering out hardwired profanities on respected media platforms, I've identified a fellow traveller. I'm thankful for Blaine's brave articulations and his bold and provocative style – one could say, a style firmly within Australia's traditions of fierce, democratic, egalitarian cultural expression and worthy of keeping alive. Here's to many more contributions to a stumbling nation reconciling with itself.

Alison Pennington

TOP BLOKES

Correspondence

Shannon Burns

After reading Lech Blaine's excellent and illuminating essay, I found myself thinking about notions of authenticity, impersonation and larrikinism as they apply to the so-called working class. Of course, some working-class people embody every cliché about working-class life, and there are others who are barely recognisable as working class to those who haven't been exposed to its diverse manifestations. As with any group, some of its members are easy to read because their personas have been predigested, while some are almost unreadable because they represent a departure from the norm and others actively reject the obvious costumes and mannerisms because contrarianism is a common impulse. Working-class people put on many uniforms and speak in many tongues.

Blaine documents the political appropriation of well-worn working-class traits or tropes and the way they are employed in the pursuit of power, and he accuses Scott Morrison of a particularly cynical and artless variety of this common act of plagiarism. "Scott Morrison's ScoMo persona was a focus-grouped act of identity theft," Blaine argues, but I'm inclined to counter that identity is always performative and that mimicry is not theft. Blaine's point is that Morrison is not authentic; part of his political strategy is to conceal his true face because his true face is not electable. He adds: "The closest that Morrison came to battling – or being a larrikin, for that matter – was getting cast as the Artful Dodger in *Oliver!*" It's a killer line, but I'm not sure that it's a killer blow. Here is a prime minister who releases images of himself making (or pretending to make) curries while listening (or pretending to listen) to a playlist entitled "Desi Hits." His theatrical impersonations, the willingness to *transparently* perform a role, seems more significant than the particular material he works with. That Morrison played such a lively and seductive part in a school musical suggests that overt theatricality is one of his organic traits, that when Morrison puts on a mask he is being his authentic self.

"Bogan Bingo" features actors who perform the role of a lower-class bingo caller. I've been to at least three performances in the past decade, all of them in the inner suburbs of Adelaide. The bingo callers pretend to be promiscuous and stupid, most of their dialogue is sexually suggestive and the action centres on the grotesque, revelling in transgression. The audience is expected to dress down as bogans and participate in various activities. This typically produces a few smoking-while-pregnant teenagers, a lot of flannel shirts and ragged jeans, ugg boots, beanies, football apparel, Iron Maiden T-shirts, mullets, references to lower-class suburbs, V8s and fast food. I've attended versions of this performance at sports clubs and schools, and in each case the audience has been primarily white-collar middle class.

It is uncomfortable to see the broad outlines of people you grew up with transformed into figures of fun – family members who *did* smoke as pregnant teenagers (like my mother and stepsister), who wore those clothes and exhibited that kind of rough and rowdy behaviour (like my younger self), people who retrospectively seem to have lived their whole lives in what others perceive as amusing costumes. That they are so easy to mimic, that the outward signs of a social group's singularity can be catalogued and repurposed with so little effort and that strangers who do not share their backgrounds or experiences can wield those signs however they like – all this is a little hard to stomach. But it is a fact worth digesting.

Part of the discomfort has to do with our relationship to the surface of things. It feels as though the people I knew and loved are being *worn* at Bogan Bingo, that the spectacle is a ghoulish possession of real bodies. But of course, they aren't part of the performance at all; their inner lives and personal histories are not attached to the cheap reproduction of those superficial traits, just as a soul is not attached to the image of a person in a photograph. It is hard to get beyond the image, to accept that imitation is not extractive and to acknowledge that the original is not diminished by insensitive reproduction just because it feels that way. But I am inclined to make the effort instead of giving in to the illusion. Nothing real is being "stolen" in these performances, and this kind of impersonation is not identity theft.

A complicating factor with Bogan Bingo is that its caricatures of lower-class and uneducated people are explicitly associated with liberation and fun. You dress down to behave in impolite and transgressive ways, to be openly unpalatable and superficial, to dance, shout and run amok and thereby taste a kind of freedom that is not usually available to you. There is an implied envy at work, a repressed desire to be a different kind of person, to strip away those middle-class masks and restraints, and become something more "real." This is not to say that those who enjoy Bogan Bingo are free of ugly beliefs or motives. Contempt for the poor and uneducated is one of the last great pleasures for inner-city progressives and conservatives alike, and I half-appreciate the openness of it all. Because this kind of "appropriation" is not yet subject to serious scrutiny or censure, we are still permitted to have fun with it, if only for now. It allows us to see how people behave before one of their tendencies becomes morally indefensible – before they learn a new set of manners and develop ways of concealing or repressing yet another impulse.

I was born into the underclass, migrated into the working class as a teenager and then settled into the middle class (via university and marriage) when I was close to thirty. I don't regard myself as an underclass or working-class writer or critic because, for me, the material conditions that people endure in the present and the social worlds they inhabit are the best guide to their class status. This belief probably says more about my origins than about the world I live in now, a world in which the "working class" is the subject of writerly analysis and political discourse instead of daily experience. "Identity" in this particular context – a context that produces things such as Quarterly Essays and the reactions they provoke – is primarily a symbolic affair, and I wonder if Blaine's strong reaction against Morrison's theatrics is a simple extension of the well-educated, middle-class sensitivity to symbols. Or to put it differently: is our hostility to Morrison's blatant imitations a sign that we don't know how to bring a lasting focus to bear on material concerns?

To my eye, Scott Morrison poses as a middle-class suburban dad. Such men drink beer, watch sport and cook food while wearing aprons. Many change personas effortlessly. One moment they are standing near the barbeque with other men talking about sport or films or women while punctuating every sentence with "fucking"; the next they are sitting down with their wives and daughters, making dad jokes while using soft gestures and polite language. The same men go to work and deploy similarly branching personas in different contexts, just as their wives present one face to their mother or siblings and other faces to their friends, neighbours, employers or employees. This morphing of character is not uncommon. In fact, it is a sign of basic social competence.

You might even say that changeability and the confident willingness to perform disparate roles is an "authentic" trait of the suburban middle class, so the question of exactly who is being impersonated when Morrison dons the supposed garments of working-class life – rugby league and beer – is tricky to determine. If middle-class people have been performing in exactly this way for decades, and if the adaptability that comes with performative prowess is one of the many sources of their confidence and success, isn't Morrison really impersonating, and thereby flattering, the middle class?

I suspect that Morrison's costumes appeal to the broader suburban middle-class more than anyone. A more interesting question, perhaps, is *who does it repel?* The answer, I think, is that a solid portion of intellectuals, writers and artsy types – people such as me – are viscerally repulsed by images of Morrison drinking beer at league games, almost as much as they are repelled by his hulking male blokeyness. Morrison doesn't bother to flatter us with imitation, perhaps because he would lose more votes than he gained. "ScoMo the typical bloke" is a steady reminder of our political irrelevance.

Blaine argues that larrikinism has its origin in forms of performance and impersonation – that Henry Lawson and Banjo Paterson were partly masking their own effeminacy or high status when they developed the anti-authoritarian larrikin figure. This is as contestable as any biographical analysis, but if we go along with it and accept that larrikinism is partly founded on deception or masking and that the "authenticity" we associate with a robust larrikin persona is an effect rather than a reality, then the business of determining exactly who is and isn't a "real" larrikin is a fool's errand.

I grew up in such safe Labor seats that voting seemed almost redundant. Even so, federal Labor victories were registered with a collective sigh of relief, and federal Labor losses had a profoundly depressing effect. The adults in my life liked Bob Hawke because he was a "character" – his larrikinism won their affection – but they also saw that he was a bullshit artist. Hawke was not one of them, and they never thought he was, yet his persona suggested that he would not regard them with contempt either, and he was prepared to tell a story and put on a show that included them in his audience. Keating left them cold.

I think that Blaine undervalues one of the most powerful qualities of the larrikin. Anti-authoritarianism and hardnosed tenacity are not the whole story. The larrikin catches your eye because his dynamism and outsized personality makes him unpredictable. He knows how to have fun and invites you along for the ride. A larrikin is playful when she is serious and serious when she is playful. He winks at you while earnestly declaring that he is a wholly honest man on serious business. The larrikin is a "character" who is capable of seducing and persuading without seeming desperate or superior. These are fundamental skills that politicians need to possess if they want to be elected, so it's not surprising that larrikinism and politics continually converge. They are made for each other.

Shannon Burns

TOP BLOKES

Correspondence

Elizabeth Flux

What's your favourite Scott Morrison nonsense phrase? Mine's "if you have a go, you get a go." To me, this sums up everything that Morrison is. It sounds catchy in passing, and if you don't interrogate them, the words seem potentially profound. But dig a bit deeper and all you find is a half-baked idea that is removed from reality.

He's saying *try and you'll succeed*.

He's saying *if you don't succeed, it's your fault*.

He's saying *responsibility lies with individuals, not society, not government and definitely not leaders*.

The problem, as Lech Blaine lays out in his essay, is that for Morrison this mantra has been true, and he therefore thinks it's universal. If you grow up thinking you're the underdog who made good, it is hard to believe anyone else has had it harder. Those worse off either don't exist or just aren't trying hard enough.

Morrison *does* get a go every time he has a go. He's failed up at every stage of his career. Now he's the prime minister, and he feels he deserves to be there – a prospect that is truly concerning because he has no insight into the reality or lived experience of the bulk of people he is supposed to represent. As Blaine summarises, "It is one thing to be lucky, and another to dedicate your life to hoarding luck from those who need some."

A leader doesn't need to have lived the lives of everyone in their constituency, but they do need to be able to see that their experience isn't the norm, that what worked for them might not work for others. It's only then that they can actually do their job – by seeing what in society needs fixing or bolstering or changing. Our government is supposed to make society work for the people, not make individuals change to fit society.

But we knew this about Morrison already. Blaine's essay underscored for me just how cynical and gross Morrison's cosplay as "ScoMo" is in light of how far removed he is from the character he is playing. After I had waded through my disgust, it also raised a lot of other questions. What does the fact that our leaders put on these costumes to curry favour with the voting public say about us?

Morrison is only the most recent – and blatant – example of politicians wearing masks. As the essay explores, it's something that happens on both sides of politics: people pretending to be something they're not ... for what reason, though? To appeal to voters, sure, but in some cases it seems to speak to something deeper.

Blaine paints a picture in which Anthony Albanese and Scott Morrison are almost pretending to be each other – "ScoMo" has adopted Albo's passions and even the form of his nickname, while Albanese (though perhaps more through social pressure than anything else) has progressively grown into the expected "image" of a politician the higher up he's got. Further back, "Hawke was desperate to be regarded as the most macho man in the country, and Keating as the smartest." Is this a grass is always greener thing? Is it about being what you are not? Is it that the public mood changed?

The essay forced me to fight against my own impressions, obtained by osmosis over the years and, until now, not interrogated or dissected. It turns out many things I thought I knew about our "top blokes" were all just surface level. What is a person's true character, then? Are politicians just amplified versions of us all, presenting our most palatable selves with more baldness and calculation? Or are our leaders' personalities produced by committee, representing a strange everyman that reflects the nation's wants at the time?

It comes back to what lies at the core of the act. Is it insecurity, or is it all a ploy to get votes and stay in power? Naturally, different people, different leaders, will fall on different parts of the spectrum. In Bob Hawke's case, it seems that his mask amplified what was already underneath, while in Morrison's, it seems he built "ScoMo" from scratch. The latter is far more frightening. What comes next for "ScoMo"? Will he just keep morphing to get what he wants?

Sometimes it is impossible to know when something is genuine and when it is performance, but I'd argue that a lot of the time it doesn't matter. I don't like inauthenticity, but if it leads to a net good, then who cares? When the act is a barrier to knowing what someone truly stands for – or whether they in fact stand for anything at all – it's a problem.

Almost everyone has an outside that differs from what's on the inside, at least a little bit. If politicians are putting on an act so they can get in power to make something happen, that's one thing. But if they're putting on an act so they can get in power just for power's sake, that's another.

As Liberal and Labor start to homogenise their policies, when they barely represent different ideologies, the parties themselves cannot represent what people want or need – this is why I think individual politicians cosplay. In theory, the leader of a party would be the embodiment of its ideals. When there are no clear ideals, the leader morphs into whoever is likely to win votes while remaining palatable to the party's base.

The scariest part of Blaine's essay is that it reveals how much rests on the charisma or personality of politicians, on people's affection for them – and that this is only getting worse. The light shines so brightly that people don't see what, if anything, lies beneath the costume. This is how we end up with hollow men with hollow promises, politicians who have personality and no policy. This is how we end up with leaders who say and believe things such as "if you have a go, you get a go," while the country burns in more ways than one.

Elizabeth Flux

TOP BLOKES

Correspondence

Tom Lee

Lech Blaine's essay is a welcome provocation to think in more nuanced ways about the complexity of Australian culture and character. Archetypes abound in the essay: the eponymous larrikin, in particular, though the bogan, aristocrat (I suppose we have them in Australia, bizarro versions like Kerry Packer), silvertail, fibro, tradie, miner, squatter, snob, cosmopolitan and parochial all get a look-in.

Blaine's greater instinct, however, is for paradox and complication, rather than settled, generic images of the nation and its constituents. As Bruce, one of his dad's best mates from Ipswich, says at one point: "I wish politicians would stop talking so much about tradies and miners ... Some of us blokes are on a coupla hundred grand. We're doing just fine. When was the last time you heard any politicians kick up a stink about the single mum cleaning the shitters at a nursing home? Or the bloke delivering Uber Eats on a bicycle for $5 a pop. That's the real working class, mate." Can you imagine the iconic, oversized thermal backpacks used by food delivery workers as the new high-vis? Matt Canavan, Bill Shorten or ScoMo donning one for a photo op on a street corner while shaking hands and getting to know the folk who wear them daily? Seems unlikely.

Cultural and financial conditions can change a lot over the generations, but off-the-shelf categories persist, shaping the stories told about the past, the analysis of the present and aspirations for the future. The metonyms "blue-" or "white-collar" capture a fragment of the worlds to which they refer in name; the more recent "laptop class" and "lentil belt" do the same. But how effective are these proxies at capturing what's important about what people do and want in Australia?

Blaine's essay shows how important political, sporting and business figures in Australia, largely men, mould themselves and in turn mould the categories that are used to define Australian aspirations and antagonisms. The end result: an unholy motley of chameleons, charlatans and spruikers, always slipping through and warping archetypes.

This raises an open question, which Blaine addresses impressionistically, without being dogmatic: what ingredients do we want to make up the important figures of the future? The journey away from deprivation to relative prosperity is for many Australian families the story of the nineteenth and twentieth centuries. But now, so-called upward mobility is looking increasingly challenging for younger Australians who don't come from home-owning families. Much change has taken place even within one generation.

This is the case for Blaine and many of his interlocutors, including Terri Butler, the member for Griffith, and Joel Thompson, a retired rugby league player of Indigenous descent and founder of The Mindset Project. Both Butler and Thompson have direct and compelling ways of describing class distinctions relevant to their upbringing. Butler describes the lives of her cousins in North Queensland as ranging from "just tough" to "really fucking tough." Thompson observes that growing up he didn't know anybody who owned their own home, making him a tad different in material circumstances from Morrison, who in 2018, according to Blaine, described himself as starting out "very, very small" on entering the property market, when in truth, "small" meant owning two houses in Bronte.

That Morrison might be perceived by the public to share common ground with the likes of Butler and Thompson on the basis of culture, largely via rugby league and a cultivated lack of pretension, could matter more in the end than whether or not he shares a common origin. The relationship between the authenticity of origins, a relatively recently acquired yet nonetheless genuine symbolic solidarity with the working class, and a strategic misleading of the public – this is the very tricky-to-map and ultimately unresolved mess that Blaine traces.

I've got to dig deep to connect with anything like "tough" or "really fucking tough." Yet like many Australians, I'm a bastard form with mixed trimmings, able to select which parts of my history to brandish, a luxury in itself. I came from Protestantism (Dad) and Catholicism (Mum), private school (Dad) and public school (Mum), the upper-middle class (Dad) and the lower-middle-to-middle class (Mum). Far from the most heady of contrasts, but enough to create some tensions.

I prized the rugby league heritage on Mum's side in my teens while attending a rich, all-boys boarding school in Sydney, taking perverse delight in being on the outer. But it was hardly the outer: State of Origin was the only weeknight of the year that we didn't have to do enforced prep after dinner. Everyone loved it.

The performance of a particularly rugged version of masculinity was the norm at the school: speaking in the harsh, monosyllabic drawl most likely learnt from farm workers, wearing shearers' singlets, smoking rollies, cutting the toes and backs off our joggers to make a sort of thong (nicknamed "Shane and Waynes"). The greatest aspiration of many was to own a B&S-ready ute with all the roo-shooting, circle-working trimmings. Stupidity was certainly the currency, rather than sensitivity or intellect. A peculiar mix of cowboy and bogan commanded, on balance, more respect than the yachtsman, the preppy, the skater or, certainly, the hipster. Everyone tended to gravitate towards larrikin types who were a bit rough around the edges. There were niches for most, although it was certainly not the happiest time for all.

I felt immense relief when I spent my gap year working at an equally elite boarding school in the United Kingdom, a co-ed school where art, music, drama and a greater level of emotional sensitivity were the norm among students. It seemed like heaven. Though perhaps I was seeing everything through the romance of my own newfound freedom and the novelty of travel.

As for ScoMo, Blaine makes a lot of the love of rugby league he seems to have developed relatively late in life (as late as 2012) and brandished as part of his political self-image. There is something cringe-worthy about the idea that Morrison is just supporting the Sharks because he knows it will play well with a section of the electorate. But perhaps we should entertain the idea that he has come to love league, like his God, and while it might be politically convenient for him to do so, he's going to games in the same way he's going to church – a good Christian, buying the hat and the scarf.

Morrison's greater crime might be that he is at best naive to the extent of his own hardship. This is Blaine's broader point concerning authenticity: if you've always done alright for money, just admit it or try to have some perspective. If you've decided to be a Sharks fan because you want people to like you, fair play, but be straight about it. Perhaps this is terrible advice from a political perspective, but I like the sound of it.

Climate change looms in Blaine's essay as a complex and divisive issue concerning class and perceived cosmopolitan elitism in Australia – a government-killer, since Abbott at least. It reminded me of a story I heard from my dad …

Dad is driving along one of the gravel roads at home and encounters a local lad, let's call him Morgan, chopping wood by the side of the road. Morgan is an old primary school friend of mine, from Cumnock town, not the landed elite, who has returned to the district as an adult. Morgan certainly had an upbringing that was challenging compared to my own. I lost touch with him when I went away to boarding school, as I did with many of my local friends.

Dad, who's become something of a local climate-change advocate, warns Morgan that he is breaking the law, that fallen branches are valuable habitat and provide soil nutrients. Morgan obediently packs up his kit and probably goes to get his wood somewhere else on the side of the road.

Whenever I remind Dad of this story, it presents him with a moral difficulty. A robust family argument tends to ensue. Dad and my brother chop firewood on our land and it's legal to do so; sometimes people ask if they can come onto the property and do the same, and permission tends to be granted. But if lots more people started asking, Dad would certainly start saying no. Our family has access and rights to a massive portion of the countryside and all the work and leisure that affords, largely because of the time my ancestors arrived in the country, as well as other rolls of the dice and, no doubt, a fair amount of sacrifice, skulduggery and nous on their part – it would be churlish of me to imagine they were without ingenuity.

But how must this feel for Morgan, less well-off, prevented from chopping the wood he needs over winter in the name of biodiversity? I know Dad feels this as a profound moral quandary. Not so Mum, who isn't from the landed gentry despite now owning the land. She doesn't feel the class guilt that Dad does, and even though Mum's arguably less of an advocate for biodiversity (despite doing plenty of practical work), she appears less conflicted laying down the law, hypothetically, to Morgan chopping wood by the side of the road.

This story is a parable because it so neatly illustrates the relationship between key progressive issues of the day, including climate change and class. Is it fair that those with existing privileges accrue more capital, both social and financial, when politics demands a shift in the trajectory of industry and the economy? How can we ensure people like Morgan have equitable access to a comfortable life without having long-lasting detrimental effects on the environment? Is it fair that some are forced to commit crimes against the environment in full view, while others can do the same things, at scale, inconspicuously and often to their financial advantage? And alternatively, should class guilt impact moral authority?

No answers from me here, merely a story to help frame the problem. This is also the value of Blaine's similarly personal but far more expansive essay. I wouldn't be surprised if it becomes a touchstone in the current political climate.

Tom Lee

TOP BLOKES

Correspondence

Vivian Gerrand

Top Blokes powerfully elucidates how, under successive Australian governments, the super-wealthy have been aided to feather their nests, while inequality and precarity have quietly grown to encompass new sectors of society.

Blaine's illumination of how class operates in Australia is compelling. It would have been even more compelling had he engaged with what precarity has meant for different sectors – and, indeed, for the intelligentsia itself.

In contemporary Australia, plumbers earn more than most professors. The "culture war" on so-called elites, many of whom are living on casual wages despite their many qualifications, has produced a new underclass. Previously secure arenas of employment – schools and universities – have become increasingly insecure. This has coincided with the precipitous rise identified in Blaine's essay in the cost of housing, unmatched by wage growth.

Reflecting upon the Labor Party's loss of the past three federal elections, Blaine memorably writes: "The terrible truth is that the cosmopolitans can afford to lose. Many make a living from faking outrage at the Establishment that by and large they belong to. The right do whatever is necessary to gain and hold power, while the left prefer virtuous defeats to imperfect victories."

While this may be true in select quarters, it obscures the diabolical impacts of precarious work and unaffordable housing on my highly educated generation, many of whom have PhDs. Education, as was pointed out by Tanya Plibersek in her response to Quarterly Essay 82, has been devalued in this country. The asymmetry between the cosmopolitans and the mythologised battler class that Blaine vividly depicts has shifted with the advent of these conditions.

This has only intensified during the Covid-19 pandemic, with Josh Frydenberg and Scott Morrison deliberately excluding universities and the arts from the Job-Keeper scheme in 2020. Fragmentation and decimation of academic and arts communities have been the predictable result. That same year, instead of tackling the housing crisis, HomeBuilder grants allocated taxpayer funds to a reno-ready demographic, bolstering support for construction – one of the few industries that has been largely unaffected by lockdowns. The expansion of homelessness is yet another predictable consequence of this policy failure.

Just last week, my university announced a further round of redundancies. A friend now needs to reapply for his job, knowing that he is up against his colleague. One of them will be the loser. The levels of stress that my generation continues to experience from job insecurity and housing unaffordability get in the way of attempts to redress injustice more broadly. In my area of research, we focus on ever-urgent issues to do with social inclusion. The fact that many of us face barriers to such inclusion, including personal precarity, reduces our capacity to act in solidarity with the broader cause.

In the next election, as in the last one, cosmopolitans cannot afford to lose.

Vivian Gerrand

TOP BLOKES

Response to Correspondence

Lech Blaine

In September, I felt the country beginning to splinter as Clive Palmer's anti-lockdown propaganda kicked into overdrive. I know lots of people in regional Queensland with zero history of vaccine hesitancy who were becoming gripped by conspiracy theories. If they felt so ferociously about lockdowns, what would the mood be like in Western Sydney and Melbourne, as a high baseline of distrust in government combined with a genuine sense of economic threat?

The answer came during the so-called tradie protests. Riot police were girt by high-vis construction workers who wanted to hit Dictator Dan where it hurt: by losing work, and potentially infecting each other with Covid.

Outside the CFMEU offices, the angry mob bombarded John Setka with accusations of betrayal. On the West Gate Bridge, the protestors sang "The Horses" by Daryl Braithwaite. *That's the way it's gonna be, little daaarlin'!* The next day, fake tradies and makeshift nationalists converged on the war memorial to shotgun pre-mixed liquor, snort Class A drugs, and chant "Advance Australia Fair".

Reports surfaced that the workers had been infiltrated by neo-Nazis. Counter-reports maintained that true-blue CFMEU members were mostly responsible. Either way, it was a grimly familiar spectacle in Australian history: larrikins suffering from an inarticulate nihilism groped around for the charade of mateship and patriotism to justify their self-destructiveness.

The protestors evoked the textbook larrikins described by David Hunt in his characteristically witty correspondence to *Top Blokes*:

> While most nineteenth-century larrikins had "working-class" backgrounds ... they loathed the labour movement, and the emerging trade unions loathed them in return. Larrikins disrupted union parades and pickets, hurling abuse and rotten food at the

marching or striking workers. Causing mayhem at union picnics was a favourite larrikin sport.

Hunt takes issue with the historical fidelity of the larrikin in my essay, and I don't blame him. As a historian, I'm not fit to shine David's shoes. I'm more interested in the myth of larrikinism that Australian politics has inherited than the literal inner-city larrikins of the 1800s.

My point wasn't that Paterson and Lawson were bona fide larrikins, but that they played a pivotal role in disseminating the myths we still cling to. Likewise, nobody would sanctify Scott Morrison as a bona fide larrikin, partly because he has zero sense of humour. But his ScoMo persona is heavily influenced by the myths of larrikinism. Larrikins such as my brother John immediately see and hear a fellow traveller. Morrison conveys to a certain cohort of voters that he will fight against the political correctness Sky News believes is killing our national hero.

Not long after the tradie riots, John Elliott died. Figures from the right and left united to describe him as a "larrikin," a euphemism often wheeled out on the death of disgraced businessmen. In the 1980s, Elliott belonged to a coterie of right-wing white-collar mavericks that included John Singleton and Alan Bond. They loved sport and beer, and made politically incorrect faux pas about women. This made them seem like mates, rather than vulture capitalists.

Increasingly, I've noticed the figure of the larrikin highlighted by culture warriors on the right as a defence against political correctness. This reactionary larrikin bears little resemblance to Hunt's textbook larrikin, or the egalitarian larrikins – of both genders – celebrated by Alison Pennington. The myth-makers link a series of contradictory figures whose common feature is that they hearken back to an idealised – and less socially progressive – time in Australia's history. It also happens to be a time when the transgressions of men went unchallenged.

In hindsight, I could have done a better job of clarifying these competing larrikins at the outset, although I reckon Shannon Burns is probably right: the business of determining exactly who is and isn't a "real" larrikin might be a fool's errand. Flicking somewhat flippantly between historical scenes was meant to convey the mess of Australian national identity, and the way we frequently use the same descriptions and categories for people who are spiritually and politically opposed. I definitely should have provided a more succinct definition of what it means to *be* a larrikin, then and now, especially in a positive sense.

Burns does a stellar job of pinpointing charismatic aspects of a larrikin:

> The larrikin catches your eye because his dynamism and outsized personality makes him unpredictable. He knows how to have fun and invites you along for the ride. A larrikin is playful when she is serious and serious when she is playful. He winks at you while earnestly declaring that he is a wholly honest man on serious business. The larrikin is a "character" who is capable of seducing and persuading without seeming desperate or superior.

I wish I'd written this. Burns could be describing my father. Dad was a Grade Eight drop-out who once upon a time worked at an abattoir while belonging to a gang of bodgies in hardscrabble Ipswich. After a serious workplace injury, he moved through various jobs, including professional gambling, dalmatian breeding and driving taxis, always hustling for money. He maintained a deep mischievous streak after becoming a publican. But there was always a warmth to his piss-takes, and he was consistently the target of his own scorn. The open advertisement of personal imperfections invited others to loosen up.

In her correspondence, former state Labor MP Rachel Nolan fleshes out the rich tradition of labourism in my father's hometown of Ipswich:

> in 1888, Australia's first Labor MP emerged from Ipswich when Thomas Glassey, a coalmining unionist [described] himself as "independent Labor" ... From 1915 to 1948, the workers of Ipswich were represented by Frank Cooper, an eight-hour-day campaigner who became treasurer in the reforming government of William Forgan Smith. Elected in 1932, that government rejected the austerity of the Premiers' Plan, rebuilt Queensland in Art Deco style and entrenched the state as the highest-wage, highest-taxing jurisdiction in the country.

This atmosphere provided the sincerely egalitarian side of my father's larrikinism. The son of a trade unionist, he was a foster parent for almost thirty years. He also must've been one of the only publicans in the country who waged personal war against WorkChoices, because he believed that the government should protect the penalty rates of his employees and customers. And – along with former Ipswich Jets coach Tommy Raudonikis – he had a profound influence on the nefarious tendencies of his nephew Allan Langer, who would become widely beloved as Queensland's number one public larrikin.

Growing up, I worshipped larrikin athletes such as Langer and Shane Warne for the same reason my father preferred Doug Walters to Don Bradman. It wasn't just their athletic prowess that enchanted. They sounded like me, a bogan with a thick Australian drawl. There were increasingly few areas of public life where I saw my identity represented unironically, or where I could look without feeling in some way substandard by comparison.

I was delighted to receive Pennington's erudite attention to gaps in my essay, and her personal identification with some of my experiences:

> As a working-class woman straddling worlds, "suffocating from class consciousness," still filtering out hardwired profanities on respected media platforms, I've identified a fellow traveller.

My brother John and I aren't biologically related, but we are cut from the same cloth. His shame caused him to identify with John Howard, who appealed to people sick of feeling like they weren't enough. As a teenager in country Queensland, my shame caused me to identify with urban elites, although I had much more in common with John on most matters except politics.

I've long since made peace with my bogan roots. Still, one of my missions as an essayist is to capture the perspective of self-identifying outsiders like John. Not because I agree with everything that he believes, but because John's beliefs are extremely popular. He isn't really an outsider. There are more of him than me. Bri Lee writes about the geographic distance between Australia's media class and the cohort of unseen voters now known as Scott Morrison's Quiet Australians, highlighted by the 2019 election:

> Everyone was acting shocked by the results coming out of Queensland, but it had been a long time since anyone actually asked Queenslanders what they wanted and stuck around to listen to the answers … It's rare to see anyone from Cairns, Townsville, Bundaberg or Rockhampton on the ABC, and certainly not on *The Drum*, where everyone sat, apparently confounded that they didn't know their compatriots.

The great irony – which I perhaps didn't explore for fear of being self-absorbed – is that by pursuing a career in writing and journalism, I'm at great risk of squandering my father's class advancements. Indeed, my brother John earns significantly more money than me, and nobody would accuse him of being an elite. I ain't complaining, because I knew what I was getting into.

But Vivian Gerrand does have a point in her correspondence:

> It would have been even more compelling had he engaged with what precarity has meant for different sectors – and, indeed, for the intelligentsia itself. In contemporary Australia, plumbers earn more than most professors. The "culture war" on so-called elites, many of whom are living on casual wages despite their many qualifications, has produced a new underclass.

I've been incredibly lucky since publishing *Top Blokes* to generate positive feedback and vehement disagreement, frequently within the same breath. Some have asked why I care if Morrison is a fraud. The best politicians are bullshit artists, and all human beings are inauthentic to some extent. It is impossible to be the same person all the time, and social media has allowed human beings to be several different people at once. As Elizabeth Flux notes:

> Sometimes it is impossible to know when something is genuine and when it is performance, but I'd argue that a lot of the time it doesn't matter. I don't like inauthenticity, but if it leads to a net good, then who cares?

My memoir, *Car Crash*, analysed the several different identities I oscillated between as a teenager. The epiphany wasn't picking just one but becoming comfortable with my contradictions. So why do I care so much about ScoMo's? Principally, I think his reinvention is interesting on a human level. It also explains something fundamental about our national identity and the changing voting bases of the major parties. Tom Lee somewhat interprets the bee in my bonnet:

> Morrison's greater crime might be that he is at best naive to the extent of his own hardship. This is Blaine's broader point concerning authenticity: if you've always done alright for money, just admit it or try to have some perspective. If you've decided to be a Sharks fan because you want people to like you, fair play, but be straight about it.

I wouldn't have such an issue with Morrison's careerist reinvention as a suburban rugby league fan if he didn't frequently seek to force Australians to conform to a narrow version of Australian identity, or to exclude people who don't from political debates. Anyone who disagrees with the government from the left, especially on climate change, is likely to be labelled as an inner-city elite. But there are no more powerful "inner-city elites" than the ones Morrison used to rub shoulders with at rugby union games or Liberal Party fundraisers. And if you seek to police public debate with stringent identity markers, you should expect your own carefully focus-grouped identity to be scrutinised.

At the same time, I didn't want the essay simply to be a critique of Scott Morrison and Coalition voters. It takes two to tango. The reason so many Australians find ScoMo's unpretentiousness appealing is because they generally feel contempt emanating from members of the media and political classes, especially progressives. Morrison embraces them unconditionally.

It remains to be seen whether a Johnny-come-lately love of beer and rugby league can save Morrison from the wrath of battlers in 2022. The prime minister has lost support among female voters, probably owing to his mishandling of the Brittany Higgins affair. This explained his puzzling appearance at the height of the Higgins cover-up to chug a beer in the dressing sheds of the Parramatta Eels, a rugby league team that he doesn't even support. Morrison wants to compensate for the loss of women by attracting blokes anxious about woke feminists.

The Coalition's game plan for the 2022 election will be similar to the last one. Morrison needs his incompetence to be eclipsed by infighting between voters who should be economic allies. At the eleventh hour, the main person responsible for the fear and loathing will present himself as a down-to-earth bloke who can unify the nation, deliver economic stability and defend larrikins from political correctness. And there is still every chance that this will work. Although I do think that "Albo" is much savvier than many pundits give him credit for, and not just because he's a South Sydney Rabbitohs fan.

Lech Blaine

Lech Blaine is the author of the memoir *Car Crash* and the Quarterly Essay *Top Blokes*. His writing has appeared in *The Monthly*, *Guardian Australia*, *The Best Australian Essays*, *Griffith Review*, *Kill Your Darlings* and *Meanjin*.

Shannon Burns is a literary critic and essayist, and a member of the J.M. Coetzee Centre for Creative Practice at the University of Adelaide. His most recent work has appeared in *Australian Book Review*, *Meanjin* and *The Sydney Review of Books*.

Elizabeth Flux's essays and feature articles have been published in *The Saturday Paper*, *Guardian Australia*, *Meanjin* and *Island*.

Vivian Gerrand is a research fellow at Deakin University and a chief investigator on the Horizon 2020 BRaVE (Building Resilience against Violent Extremism and Polarisation) project. She is the author of *Possible Spaces of Somali Belonging*.

Jess Hill is an investigative journalist and the author of *See What You Made Me Do*. She has been a producer for ABC Radio and a journalist for *Background Briefing*, and Middle East correspondent for *The Global Mail*. *See What You Made Me Do* won the 2020 Stella Prize and the ABA Booksellers' Choice Adult Non-Fiction Book of the Year.

David Hunt is the author of the Unauthorised History of Australia series: *Girt*, *True Girt* and the recently released *Girt Nation*.

Bri Lee is an academic and activist, and the author of *Who Gets to Be Smart*, *Beauty* and *Eggshell Skull*. Her journalism has appeared in *The Monthly*, *The Saturday Paper*, *Guardian Australia* and *Crikey*.

Tom Lee researches the relationship between narrative and technology in the School of Design at the University of Technology Sydney. His first novel, *Coach Fitz*, was published in 2019. His second novel, *Object Coach*, is due out in 2022.

Rachel Nolan is the co-chair of the McKell Institute in Queensland and consults to Southeast Asian governments on public administration through the University of Queensland. She was the state member for Ipswich in the Queensland parliament from 2001 to 2012 and held the portfolios of Transport, Natural Resources, Finance and the Arts as part of Anna Bligh's Labor government.

Alison Pennington is a senior economist at the Australia Institute's Centre for Future Work. She conducts research on economic issues facing working people, including the future of jobs, skills and the role of government.

20 YEARS OF QUARTERLY ESSAY

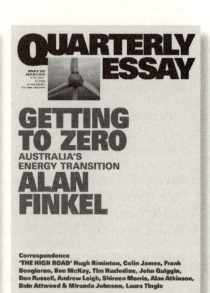

Subscribe to the Friends of Quarterly Essay email newsletter to share in news, updates, events and special offers as we celebrate our 20th anniversary.

quarterlyessay.com.au/signup

QUARTERLY ESSAY
BACK ISSUES

BACK ISSUES: (Prices include GST, postage and handling within Australia.) *Grey indicates out of stock.*

- ☐ QE 1 ($17.99) Robert Manne *In Denial*
- ☐ QE 2 ($17.99) John Birmingham *Appeasing Jakarta*
- ☐ QE 3 ($17.99) Guy Rundle *The Opportunist*
- ☐ QE 4 ($17.99) Don Watson *Rabbit Syndrome*
- ☐ QE 5 ($17.99) Mungo MacCallum *Girt By Sea*
- ☐ QE 6 ($17.99) John Button *Beyond Belief*
- ☐ QE 7 ($17.99) John Martinkus *Paradise Betrayed*
- ☐ QE 8 ($17.99) Amanda Lohrey *Groundswell*
- ☐ QE 9 ($17.99) Tim Flannery *Beautiful Lies*
- ☐ QE 10 ($17.99) Gideon Haigh *Bad Company*
- ☐ QE 11 ($17.99) Germaine Greer *Whitefella Jump Up*
- ☐ QE 12 ($17.99) David Malouf *Made in England*
- ☐ QE 13 ($17.99) Robert Manne with David Corlett *Sending Them Home*
- ☐ QE 14 ($17.99) Paul McGeough *Mission Impossible*
- ☐ QE 15 ($17.99) Margaret Simons *Latham's World*
- ☐ QE 16 ($17.99) Raimond Gaita *Breach of Trust*
- ☐ QE 17 ($17.99) John Hirst *'Kangaroo Court'*
- ☐ QE 18 ($17.99) Gail Bell *The Worried Well*
- ☐ QE 19 ($17.99) Judith Brett *Relaxed & Comfortable*
- ☐ QE 20 ($17.99) John Birmingham *A Time for War*
- ☐ QE 21 ($17.99) Clive Hamilton *What's Left?*
- ☐ QE 22 ($17.99) Amanda Lohrey *Voting for Jesus*
- ☐ QE 23 ($17.99) Inga Clendinnen *The History Question*
- ☐ QE 24 ($17.99) Robyn Davidson *No Fixed Address*
- ☐ QE 25 ($17.99) Peter Hartcher *Bipolar Nation*
- ☐ QE 26 ($17.99) David Marr *His Master's Voice*
- ☐ QE 27 ($17.99) Ian Lowe *Reaction Time*
- ☐ QE 28 ($17.99) Judith Brett *Exit Right*
- ☐ QE 29 ($17.99) Anne Manne *Love & Money*
- ☐ QE 30 ($17.99) Paul Toohey *Last Drinks*
- ☐ QE 31 ($17.99) Tim Flannery *Now or Never*
- ☐ QE 32 ($17.99) Kate Jennings *American Revolution*
- ☐ QE 33 ($17.99) Guy Pearse *Quarry Vision*
- ☐ QE 34 ($17.99) Annabel Crabb *Stop at Nothing*
- ☐ QE 35 ($17.99) Noel Pearson *Radical Hope*
- ☐ QE 36 ($17.99) Mungo MacCallum *Australian Story*
- ☐ QE 37 ($17.99) Waleed Aly *What's Right?*
- ☐ QE 38 ($17.99) David Marr *Power Trip*
- ☐ QE 39 ($17.99) Hugh White *Power Shift*
- ☐ QE 40 ($17.99) George Megalogenis *Trivial Pursuit*
- ☐ QE 41 ($17.99) David Malouf *The Happy Life*
- ☐ QE 42 ($17.99) Judith Brett *Fair Share*
- ☐ QE 43 ($17.99) Robert Manne *Bad News*
- ☐ QE 44 ($17.99) Andrew Charlton *Man-Made World*
- ☐ QE 45 ($17.99) Anna Krien *Us and Them*
- ☐ QE 46 ($17.99) Laura Tingle *Great Expectations*
- ☐ QE 47 ($17.99) David Marr *Political Animal*
- ☐ QE 48 ($17.99) Tim Flannery *After the Future*
- ☐ QE 49 ($17.99) Mark Latham *Not Dead Yet*
- ☐ QE 50 ($17.99) Anna Goldsworthy *Unfinished Business*
- ☐ QE 51 ($17.99) David Marr *The Prince*
- ☐ QE 52 ($17.99) Linda Jaivin *Found in Translation*
- ☐ QE 53 ($17.99) Paul Toohey *That Sinking Feeling*
- ☐ QE 54 ($17.99) Andrew Charlton *Dragon's Tail*
- ☐ QE 55 ($17.99) Noel Pearson *A Rightful Place*
- ☐ QE 56 ($17.99) Guy Rundle *Clivosaurus*
- ☐ QE 57 ($17.99) Karen Hitchcock *Dear Life*
- ☐ QE 58 ($17.99) David Kilcullen *Blood Year*
- ☐ QE 59 ($17.99) David Marr *Faction Man*
- ☐ QE 60 ($17.99) Laura Tingle *Political Amnesia*
- ☐ QE 61 ($17.99) George Megalogenis *Balancing Act*
- ☐ QE 62 ($17.99) James Brown *Firing Line*
- ☐ QE 63 ($17.99) Don Watson *Enemy Within*
- ☐ QE 64 ($17.99) Stan Grant *The Australian Dream*
- ☐ QE 65 ($17.99) David Marr *The White Queen*
- ☐ QE 66 ($17.99) Anna Krien *The Long Goodbye*
- ☐ QE 67 ($17.99) Benjamin Law *Moral Panic 101*
- ☐ QE 68 ($17.99) Hugh White *Without America*
- ☐ QE 69 ($17.99) Mark McKenna *Moment of Truth*
- ☐ QE 70 ($17.99) Richard Denniss *Dead Right*
- ☐ QE 71 ($17.99) Laura Tingle *Follow the Leader*
- ☐ QE 72 ($17.99) Sebastian Smee *Net Loss*
- ☐ QE 73 ($17.99) Rebecca Huntley *Australia Fair*
- ☐ QE 74 ($17.99) Erik Jensen *The Prosperity Gospel*
- ☐ QE 75 ($17.99) Annabel Crabb *Men at Work*
- ☐ QE 76 ($17.99) Peter Hartcher *Red Flag*
- ☐ QE 77 ($17.99) Margaret Simons *Cry Me a River*
- ☐ QE 78 ($17.99) Judith Brett *The Coal Curse*
- ☐ QE 79 ($17.99) Katharine Murphy *The End of Certainty*
- ☐ QE 80 ($17.99) Laura Tingle *The High Road*
- ☐ QE 81 ($24.99) Alan Finkel *Getting to Zero*
- ☐ QE 82 ($24.99) George Megalogenis *Exit Strategy*
- ☐ QE 83 ($24.99) Lech Blaine *Top Blokes*

Please include this form with delivery and payment details overleaf.
Back issues also available as eBooks at **quarterlyessay.com**

SUBSCRIBE TO RECEIVE
10% OFF THE COVER PRICE

☐ **ONE-YEAR PRINT AND DIGITAL SUBSCRIPTION: $89.99**

- Print edition × 4
- Home delivery
- Full digital access to all past issues, including downloadable eBook files
- Access iPad & iPhone app
- Access Android app

DELIVERY AND PAYMENT DETAILS

DELIVERY DETAILS:

NAME:

ADDRESS:

EMAIL: PHONE:

PAYMENT DETAILS: Enclose a cheque/money order made out to Schwartz Books Pty Ltd.
Or debit my credit card (MasterCard, Visa and Amex accepted).
Freepost: Quarterly Essay, Reply Paid 90094, Carlton VIC 3053
All prices include GST, postage and handling.

CARD NO.

EXPIRY DATE: /   CCV: AMOUNT: $

PURCHASER'S NAME: SIGNATURE:

Subscribe online at **quarterlyessay.com/subscribe** • Freecall: 1800 077 514 • Phone: 03 9486 0288
Email: subscribe@quarterlyessay.com (please do not send electronic scans of this form)